Biblical Discipleship Study Guide

Essential Components for Attaining Spiritual Maturity

Biblical Discipleship Study Guide

Essential Components for

Attaining Spiritual Maturity

Todd M. Fink

Biblical Discipleship Study Guide

Essential Components for Attaining Spiritual Maturity

by
Todd M. Fink

Published by Selah Book Press

Cover Illustration Copyright © 2016 by Selah Book Press
Cover design by Selah Book Press

ISBN-10: 1944601058
ISBN-13: 978-1-944601-05-8

First Edition

ABBREVIATIONS

ESV	English Standard Version
NIV	New International Version
NKJV	New King James Version
NASB	New American Standard Bible
NET	New English Translation

Endorsements

As president of a Bible college and seminary, I am regularly asked if there is a discipleship book that I can strongly recommend. Thanks to Todd M. Fink, I finally have an answer. *Biblical Discipleship* addresses one of the greatest needs in the modern church. It takes into account the current cultural situation and the effects of bad theology, while suggesting practical strategies for personal growth. This book is, no doubt, going to push the ball forward.

— Dr. Braxton Hunter, Ph.D. President of Trinity
    Theological Seminary

To be a Christian is to be a disciple. To grow as a Christian demands pursuing the life of discipleship. Todd M. Fink has devoted his life to cross-cultural ministry and helping people know and grow in Christ. His many years of experience in the ministry and devotion to the Scriptures have made him a man with great wisdom on this vital topic. I'm thankful he has written this helpful resource to help God's people grow.

— Dr. Erik Thoennes, Ph.D. Professor of Theology/Chair
    Undergraduate Theology at Biola University/Talbot
    School of Theology; Pastor at Grace Evangelical Free
    Church, La Mirada, California

Todd M. Fink's *Biblical Discipleship: Essential Components for Attaining Spiritual Maturity* will prove to be a valuable resource to many who are interested in growing a deeper devotion to Christ. Fink opines an analysis of the major problems/issues in the contemporary Evangelical church that he believes are hindrances to a healthy discipleship focus. He offers a corrective vision for those who desire to go against this Evangelical sub-culture, as he describes it, and be faithful to God's call on their lives.

— Dr. David Talley, Ph.D. Professor/Chair Old Testament
    Department, Biola University

Table of Contents

Foreword

By Dr. Braxton Hunter, Ph.D.

Much of the modern church is spiritually malnourished. Contributing to this daunting dilemma are the realities of neglected, theologically corrupt, poorly devised, half-hearted and shallow forms of what some call discipleship. This is not an overstatement.

If it's not the result of an obvious human effort to distort the Christian teaching, much of the blame rests with the Western Evangelical proclivity to offer a consumer-driven church experience. Rather than choosing a local congregation based on doctrinal perspectives and spiritual growth possibilities, it's now common for individuals to join an assembly because of the amenities it offers. This sort of thinking has been suggested to the community by the local church herself. "Come visit us. We have a great _____!" One can fill in the blank with any number of services or benefits: praise band, exercise classes, gymnasium, coffee bar, and so on. It's not that there's anything wrong with these things. It's just that many local congregations have entered into an invisible contract with the community that says, "We are valuable, primarily because of these benefits," instead of one that says, "We will train you in the truth."

In other cases, the reason for this poor spiritual diet is spiritual fatigue. It seems hard enough for church leaders to care for the needs of a congregation of believers. Doing proper discipleship and training congregants to disciple each other is a time-consuming project that requires great effort and discernment. This hindrance is particularly the case for ministry leaders and churches in ministry contexts that require the majority

1

of their efforts to be spent on evangelism. However, a proper emphasis on discipleship can bolster those other efforts. More discipleship breeds more servants and more evangelism.

Nevertheless, it is often the case that the lack of rich and robust discipleship is because of an ignorance of how to accomplish it. Simply put, many ministry leaders and individuals need specific instruction on this vital matter. What they ultimately need is an explanation of how to reach spiritual maturity in their lives.

Fortunately, Todd M. Fink has provided us with just that. Though the shelves of Christian bookstores are replete with discipleship training materials, *Biblical Discipleship* is a welcome addition. It is unique in its clarity and insight. As a practical minister and an academic, I consider this book to be required reading.

Dr. Braxton Hunter, Ph.D.
President of Trinity Theological Seminary

Introduction

Today, we have many ways of defining success in life. Some define it as being a sports hero, others as being wealthy, others as being popular and well liked, and still others as being happy. How does God define success? He defines it as being spiritually mature!

How do we become spiritually mature? There's only one way, and it's called discipleship. However, statistics show that discipleship is in a state of crisis today. Many Christians are not growing in Christ and are stuck in the process of reaching spiritual maturity. A Barna study reveals that almost nine out of ten senior pastors of Protestant churches assert that spiritual immaturity is one of the most serious issues facing the church.[1]

Sadly, what discipleship meant in the time of Christ and what it means today is vastly different. Moreover, the importance Christ and the Apostles gave to discipleship is also stunningly different than the importance many Christians and churches today give it.

Unlike the disciples who had much of Scripture memorized, a whopping 81% of Christians today don't read their Bibles regularly. Unlike Christ's disciples who were "Fishers of Men," 61% of believers today have not shared their faith in the past six months. And sadly, unlike Christ and the Apostles who made discipleship the central focus of their ministries, 81% of pastors today have no regular discipleship programs in their churches. Discipleship is being neglected today and the consequences are crippling many Christians and churches. This book study hopes to change that!

---

[1] C. S. Lewis Institute, *Sparking a Discipleship Movement in America and Beyond,* cslewisinstitute.org, http://www.cslewisinstitute.org/webfm_send/210, Accessed 08/19/2015.

Discipleship is a command for all believers and is our highest calling. This study guide provides biblical help for fulfilling this calling and seeks to discover what God says about genuine growth in Christ. It's both an informative and "how-to" study guide that offers practical help for overcoming the barriers that stand in the way of attaining spiritual maturity.

This study guide is taken from the book *Biblical Discipleship: Essential Components for Attaining Spiritual Maturity.* In order to get a larger perspective on discipleship and spiritual maturity, you are encouraged to read it as well.

God's Blessings Are Waiting!

What would change in the average Christian's life if they rightly understood the essential components of the discipleship process and practiced them? What if, instead of a single or a several-pronged approach to discipleship we addressed it from a comprehensive angle? How might our lives be changed? How might our homes be transformed? How might the church be strengthened? How might the Kingdom of God be advanced? And moreover, how might God be honored and glorified?

So, are you ready to grow? Would you like to be pleasing to God? Would you like to fulfill the reason for which you've been created? Would you like the full blessings of God in your life? Would you like to hear Christ's words, "Well done, good and faithful servant," when you arrive in heaven? If so, this book study is for you.

It's time to grow! God's blessings are waiting! Are you ready to attain them and become spiritually mature?

How to Use This Study Guide

This study guide will deal with how to apply the essential components of discipleship to your life in order to grow in Christ and attain spiritual maturity. It can be used in both a group and individual setting. If used in an individual setting, replace the discussion questions with personal reflection thoughts. For each week's session, there will be four steps (except for weeks 1 and 16).

> **Step One**: Preliminary Reading
>
> **Step Two**: Spiritual Assessment Tests to Measure Your Level of Spiritual Maturity
>
> **Step Three**: Discussion and/or Reflection Questions
>
> **Step Four**: Ideas & Goals for Growing in Spiritual Maturity

Now let's briefly look at each step:

Step One: Preliminary Reading

Before each week's meeting, you should read the preliminary reading. This will allow you to be familiar with that week's topic and be prepared to share your thoughts with the group.

Step Two: Spiritual Maturity Self-Assessment Tests

Self-assessment tests are provided for each of the essential components of discipleship in order to help you discover your spiritual maturity level in each category. God says in 2 Corinthians 13:5 to "**Examine yourselves**, to see whether you are in the faith. **Test yourselves**. Or do you not realize this about yourselves, that Jesus Christ is in you? – unless indeed, you **fail to meet the test!**"

God expects us to analyze and examine ourselves to ascertain our level of spiritual maturity. For this reason, self-assessment tests are provided for each category, and an overall spiritual maturity test can be found at the end of this study guide in week 16.

At the beginning of each section dealing with an essential component of discipleship, a short self-assessment questionnaire is provided to help you see your level of spiritual maturity in that category. Please answer the questions honestly and then ask a close loved-one to answer it for you as well. Between all responses, you should get a good idea of your level of spiritual maturity for that category.

Nature of the Questions for the Self-Assessment Tests

In order to accurately discover your spiritual maturity level in each category, the self-assessment test questions must be asked from the highest level possible or they won't provide accurate results. Therefore, the questions reflect what I believe should be the characteristics of a spiritually mature believer. There are only 10 questions per test, so there are many other great questions that could be asked but aren't.

Charts and Graphs for Visualizing and Measuring Your Spiritual Maturity Level and Growth

A chart is provided (see the following example) for each essential component of discipleship (for weeks 2-15) and shows eight stages of spiritual growth: baby, toddler, child, adolescent, teen, young adult, middle-aged adult, and mature adult.

Please note that these labels have nothing to do with your own age. For example, you could be a "mature adult" in physical age, but a "baby" in your spiritual maturity. Similarly, you could be a "teen" physically, but be a "middle-aged adult" in your spiritual maturity. These labels are used solely for the purpose of identifying your spiritual maturity level, not your physical age.

You can mark on these charts (in pencil in case you want to make changes in the future) so you can see and measure your level of spiritual maturity for each category.

Spiritual Maturity Grade from the "Example" Test

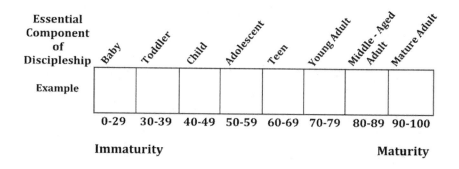

An overall spiritual maturity chart is provided for weeks 1 and 16 for your help as well (please see the chart below).

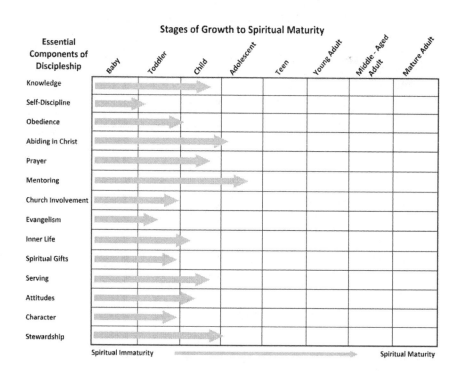

Step Three: Discussion and/or Reflection Questions

The questions are taken primarily from the preliminary reading for each week. Therefore, in order to get the most out of the discussion questions, each participant is highly encouraged to read the preliminary reading section. Everyone is encouraged to share in the discussion questions. There will be more talkative and less talkative people in the group, but the less talkative should share as much as possible. There are eight discussion questions provided for each week. If time restraints are an issue, you are welcome to choose the questions you feel are most important.

Step Four: Practical Ideas for Attaining Spiritual Maturity

After you've taken the self-assessment test for discovering your level of spiritual maturity in a particular category, then you'll find practical ideas for growth in that area. For group participation, it would be good to do this ahead of time so you can come prepared to share your plans and goals.

It's important to choose at least one of the ideas and begin doing it right away. Growth in Christ doesn't happen by merely knowing what to do, but by **doing** what we know we should do!

Week 1: Introduction to Discipleship

Step 1: Preliminary Reading

Dallas Willard, in his book *The Great Omission,* makes an incredible observation regarding the importance of discipleship when stating that the word "disciple" occurs 269 times in the New Testament, but "Christian" is only found three times.[2] Willard defines discipleship as the foundational aspect of what it means to be saved and be a true follower of Christ.

Anthony Robinson, in his article "Follow Me," picks up on Willard's statement and believes that because the word "disciple" occurs 269 times in the New Testament, it defines the mark of a genuine believer.[3] Robinson also contends that the church today is focusing primarily on conversion and neglecting the way of life here and now, which is discipleship.[4]

What Is Discipleship?

Discipleship is the process of becoming like Christ in our nature, character, values, purposes, thoughts, knowledge, attitudes, and will. In other words, it's the process of becoming spiritually mature. It lasts a lifetime and isn't relegated to a temporary study or dedicated class taken for a time and ended. Bill Hull claims, "It's not a program or an event; it's a way of life. Discipleship is not for beginners alone; it's for all believers for

---

[2] Dallas Willard, *The Great Omission* (HarperCollins, Kindle Edition, 2009-10-13), p. 3.
[3] Anthony B. Robinson, *The Renewed Focus on Discipleship: 'Follow Me'* (Christian Century, 124 no 18 S 4 2007, pp. 23-25. Publication Type: Article. ATLA Religion Database with ATLASerials. Hunter Resource Library), p. 23, Accessed 12/10/2014.
[4] Ibid., p. 23.

every day of their lives."[5]

Discipleship Is the Only Way to Spiritual Maturity

Discipleship is the vehicle God uses to make us spiritually mature. There is no other way! It's the pathway we must follow in order to be transformed into the image of Christ and reach spiritual maturity. Through discipleship, God grants us life, love, joy, peace, healthy minds, healthy relationships, healthy families, and healthy churches. It's our life's calling and the highest purpose to which we can give ourselves.

Howard Hendricks went so far as to claim, "When a person makes a profession of faith and … is never taken through a formal discipleship process, then there's little hope of seeing genuine spiritual transformation."[6]

To the degree we are committed to discipleship will be the degree to which we attain spiritual maturity. To the degree we neglect our commitment to discipleship will be the degree to which we suffer destruction, devastation, and eternal loss.

The Role of Discipleship in the Ministry of Christ

I've had the splendid privilege of standing on the mountain

 where it's believed Christ gave the Great Commission. It's called Mt. Arbel and has a spectacular view of the Sea of Galilee. It's estimated that Jesus spent 70% of His

---

[5] Bill Hull, *The Complete Book of Discipleship: On Being and Making Followers of Christ* (The Navigators Reference Library 1, 2014, NavPress, Kindle Edition), Kindle Locations 436-437.
[6] C. S. Lewis Institute, *Sparking a Discipleship Movement in America and Beyond,* cslewisinstitute.org, http://www.cslewisinstitute.org/webfm_send/210, Accessed 08/19/2015.

ministry time around the Sea of Galilee, so Mt. Arbel would have been the perfect backdrop for Christ to have spoken some of His last and most important words to His disciples: "Go therefore and make disciples of all nations, baptizing them in the name of the Father and of the Son and of the Holy Spirit, teaching them to observe all that I have commanded you. And behold, I am with you always, to the end of the age" (Matt. 28:19–20).

A large part of Christ's earthly ministry entailed making disciples. During this time, He invested heavily into 12 men. Then, upon leaving, He commanded these men to go into all the world and make disciples.

The Great Commission Mandate given by Christ contains the summation of His purpose for the original disciples and all believers for all time. It would make sense then that the essential components of the discipleship-making process should be fully understood and obeyed. Unfortunately, there appears to be an immense lack of understanding in this vital area, and the gap between the command and implementation is alarmingly wide.

The Role of Discipleship in the Ministry of the Apostles

In addition to Christ's Great Commission Mandate to make disciples, the Apostle Paul sums up his, and the other Apostles' life work with the following statement: "Him we proclaim, warning everyone and teaching everyone with all wisdom that we may **present everyone mature in Christ**. For this I toil, struggling with all his energy that he powerfully works within me" (Col. 1:28–29). This verse highlights the central purpose and work of the Apostles, which was to present every person spiritually mature in Christ.

Because presenting every person mature in Christ would logically incorporate discipleship, and because the Apostles took seriously Christ's command to make disciples, it's safe to say that the summation of the Apostles' work was discipleship as well.

Therefore, in the Great Commission, we see the summation of Christ's work and purpose, and in Colossians 1:28–29 we see the summation of the Apostles' work and purpose, each focusing on discipleship as its central theme. For this reason, the role of discipleship is paramount in the life of every believer and church, if we're going to be serious about becoming spiritually mature.

How Discipleship Is Viewed Today

Unlike the high priority Christ and the Apostles gave to discipleship, and despite Christ's command to be and make disciples, discipleship today is a low priority in the life of most churches and Christians. John Stott affirms this trend by acknowledging, "The state of the church today is marked by a paradox of growth without depth. Our zeal to go wider has not been matched by a commitment to go deeper."[7]

In the majority of churches today, discipleship is not a central focus nor are there clear strategies for making disciples taking place. A recent survey done by Richard J. Krejcir reveals that 81% of pastors have no regular discipleship program or effective effort of mentoring their people to deepen their Christian formation.[8]

Many of these churches seem to have the idea that discipleship isn't that important, or they hope it will somehow be fulfilled through preaching, Sunday School, home Bible studies, and small groups. However, most churchgoers aren't involved in all these activities, and even if they were, most of these activities aren't primarily focused on discipleship. The passion for fulfilling the commandment to make disciples through an intentional, strategic process seems to be lacking in the average Evangelical church today.

---

[7] Ibid., Accessed 08/19/2015.
[8] Richard J. Krejcir, *Statistics on Pastors: What is Going on with the Pastors in America?* 2007, www.churchleadership.org/apps/articles/default.asp?articleid=42347&columnid=4545, Accessed 08/06/2015.

When the average churchgoer is asked what the discipleship process should entail, head scratching and bewilderment sets in. David Platt shares his concern about Christians today and their understanding of discipleship: "If you ask individual Christians today what it practically means to make disciples, you will likely get jumbled thoughts, ambiguous answers, and probably even some blank stares."[9]

Many believe discipleship is optional or only applies to an elite group of radical Christians. Moreover, for the average churchgoer who does believe discipleship applies to them, most think of it as general growth that takes place through casual church attendance and occasional Scripture reading. It's not thought of as a comprehensive, intentional set of disciplines that must be seriously engaged in for discipleship to occur.

There's even significant debate regarding the essential components of the discipleship-making process among leading theologians. While there has been ample discussion and much written on the topic, there's still significant confusion surrounding what discipleship should involve.

Spiritual Maturity: the Overlooked Elephant in the Room

God's purpose for us in this life is that we would be transformed into the image of Christ: "For those whom he foreknew he also predestined to be **conformed to the image of his Son**, in order that he might be the firstborn among many brothers" (Rom. 8:29). Discipleship is how God transforms us!

Sadly, for most Christians and churches, this is not their focus. As a result, the elephant in the room (what we should be focused on) is neglected and overlooked. While becoming spiritually mature should be a believer's highest goal and priority in life, for the vast majority of Christians, becoming spiritually

---

[9] David Platt, *Follow Me* (Carol Stream, Tyndale House Publishers, 2013), p. 69.

mature isn't even on their radar screen.

The Lack of Discipleship Today

You would think that the importance of the Great Commission Mandate to make disciples (Matt. 28:19–20), and the focus on discipleship by the Apostles as the means to present every person spiritually mature in Christ (Col. 1:28–29), would bring to the forefront the importance of discipleship. However, many adversarial winds are pushing against it, and the church is in a perilous state of health as a result.

Bill Hull states, "I find it particularly puzzling that we struggle to put disciple-making at the center of ministry even though Jesus left us with the clear imperative to 'make disciples.'"[10] Again, Hull sounds out, "Let's start with the obvious. Discipleship ranks as God's top priority because Jesus practiced it and commanded us to do it, and his followers continued it."[11] However, discipleship is being neglected and discarded by many today as optional or only for the "radical believer." As a result, most Christians today are spiritually immature.

Neglected Warnings

In addition to the importance Christ and the Apostles placed on discipleship, a number of well-known pastors, authors, and theologians have sounded the alarm over the years as well. Unfortunately, their voices seem to be lost in our busy, fast-paced lifestyles.

Dietrich Bonhoeffer, in his classic work *The Cost of Discipleship*, strives to help us understand that genuine salvation

---

[10] Bill Hull, *The Complete Book of Discipleship: On Being and Making Followers of Christ* (The Navigators Reference Library 1, 2014, NavPress, Kindle Edition), Kindle Locations 441-443.
[11] Ibid., Kindle Locations 458-459.

should include discipleship. He states, "Cheap grace is the preaching of forgiveness without requiring repentance, baptism without church discipline, communion without confession, absolution without personal confession. Cheap grace is grace without discipleship, grace without the cross, grace without Jesus Christ, living and incarnate."[12]

Bonhoeffer claims that today we often exchange discipleship with emotional uplifts instead of steadfast adherence to Christ's command regarding discipleship and its role in every believer's life.[13] Bonhoeffer cries out, "If our Christianity has ceased to be serious about discipleship, if we have watered down the gospel into emotional uplift which makes no costly demands and which fails to distinguish between natural and Christian existence, then we cannot help regarding the cross as an ordinary everyday calamity, as one of the trials and tribulations of life."[14]

Dallas Willard makes the lack of discipleship a major theme in two of his books, *The Great Omission* and *The Spirit of the Disciplines*. In *The Spirit of the Disciplines*, Willard claims, "One specific errant concept has done inestimable harm to the church and God's purposes with us — and that is the concept that has restricted the Christian idea of salvation to mere forgiveness of sins."[15] Willard also makes a bold statement regarding the importance of discipleship when he declares, "I believe there is nothing wrong with the church that a clear minded resolute application of discipleship to Jesus Christ would not cure."[16]

Bill Hull has also recently weighed in on the lack of discipleship today and states, "Unfortunately, non-discipleship

---

[12] Dietrich Bonhoeffer, *The Cost of Discipleship* (SCM Classics, Hymns Ancient and Modern Ltd., Kindle Edition, 2011-08-16), Kindle Locations 604-606.
[13] Ibid., Kindle Locations 1265-1267.
[14] Ibid., Kindle Locations 1265-1267.
[15] Dallas Willard, *The Spirit of the Disciplines* (2009-02-06, HarperCollins, Kindle Edition), p. 33.
[16] Dallas Willard, *Transformed by the Renewing of the Mind* (Lecture given at Henry Center for Theological Understanding, 2012), https://youtu.be/jkzeUcnzYbM, Accessed 10/15/2015.

'Christianity' dominates much of the thinking of the contemporary church. In addition to sucking the strength from the church, Christianity without discipleship causes the church to assimilate itself into the culture. And sadly, whenever the difference between the church's and culture's definition of morality ceases to exist, the church loses its power and authority."[17]

Hull goes on to warn, "Many mainline churches depart from orthodoxy because they reject the absolute authority of Scripture. However, many Evangelical churches pose an even more subtle danger by departing from the gospel that calls on all believers to be disciples and follow Christ in obedience."[18]

George Barna is also concerned about the lack of discipleship today. He says, "My study of discipleship in America has been eye-opening. Almost every church in our country has some type of discipleship program or set of activities, but stunningly few churches have a church of disciples. Maybe that is because for many Christians today, including Christian leaders, discipleship is not terribly important. If we can get people to attend worship services, pay for the church's buildings and salaries, and muster positive, loving attitudes toward one another and toward the world, we often feel that's good enough."[19] Barna stresses, "The strength and influence of the church are wholly dependent upon its commitment to true discipleship. Producing transformed lives and seeing those lives reproduced in others is a core challenge to believers and the local church."[20]

Greg Ogden is also troubled by the lack of discipleship today;

[17] Bill Hull, *The Complete Book of Discipleship: On Being and Making Followers of Christ* (The Navigators Reference Library 1, 2014, NavPress, Kindle Edition), Kindle Locations 341-344.
[18] Ibid., Kindle Locations 341-344.
[19] George Barna, *Growing True Disciples: New Strategies for Producing Genuine Followers of Christ* (Barna Reports, p. 20, 2013, The Crown Publishing Group, Kindle Edition), p. 18.
[20] Ibid., p. 21.

he says, "If I were to choose one word to summarize the state of discipleship today, that word would be superficial. There appears to be a general lack of comprehension among many who claim Jesus as Savior as to the implications of following him as Lord."[21]

Cal Thomas, a Christian syndicated columnist and social commentator, calls on Christians to look at the quality of our discipleship instead of directing our indignation at the moral decay. He writes, "The problem in our culture isn't the abortionists. It is not the pornographers or drug dealers or criminals. It is the undisciplined, undiscipled, disobedient, and biblically ignorant Church of Jesus Christ."[22]

The Consequences of Neglecting Discipleship

The level of spiritual maturity among many Christians today is extremely concerning. This is primarily due to the misunderstanding of what discipleship entails and the neglect of an intentional, strategic plan for making disciples. While there are many positive things happening in the church today, there's a grave concern in the area of discipleship. According to recent statistics, the state of the average Christian and Evangelical church of the Western world today is in crises mode and suffering the consequences of neglecting discipleship. Consider the following stats:

- Only 19% of Christians read their Bibles daily or regularly (this means 81% don't read their Bibles daily or regularly).[23]
- About 40% of Evangelical Christians rarely or never read

---

[21]Greg Ogden, *Transforming Discipleship: Making Disciples a Few at a Time* (2010, InterVarsity Press, Kindle Edition), p. 21.
[22]Ibid., p. 22.
[23] Russ Rankin, *Study: Bible Engagement in Churchgoer's Hearts, Not Always Practiced,* Nashville, 2012, http://www.lifeway.com/Article/research-survey-bible-engagement-churchgoers, Accessed 07/23/2015.

their Bibles.[24]

- Most Christians are biblically illiterate. Fewer than half of all adults can name the four Gospels, and many Christians cannot identify more than two or three of the disciples.[25]

- Atheists, agnostics, and Mormons scored better on biblical literacy than Evangelical Christians (Pew Research).[26]

- Of self-identified Christians, 27% believe Jesus sinned while on earth (Barna).[27]

- 61% of Christians have not shared their faith in the last six months.[28]

- 48% of Christians have never invited a friend to church.[29]

- Only 25% of church members attend a Bible study or small group at least twice a month.[30]

- The average Christian prays somewhere between 1–7 minutes a day.[31]

- 81% of pastors have no regular discipleship program or effective effort of mentoring their people to deepen their Christian formation.[32]

---

[24] Ibid., Accessed 07/23/2015.

[25] Albert Mohler, *The Scandal of Biblical Illiteracy: It's Our Problem,* Christianity.com, http://www.christianity.com/1270946, Accessed 08/18/2015.

[26] C. S. Lewis Institute, *Sparking a Discipleship Movement in America and Beyond,* cslewisinstitute.org, http://www.cslewisinstitute.org/webfm_send/210, Accessed 08/19/2015.

[27] Ibid., Accessed 08/19/2015.

[28] Jon D. Wilke, *Churchgoers Believe in Sharing Faith, Most Never Do,* 2012, Lifeway.com, http://www.lifeway.com/Article/research-survey-sharing-christ-2012, Accessed 08/19/2015.

[29] Ibid., Accessed 08/04/2015.

[30] Richard J. Krejcir, *Statistics on Pastors: What is Going on with the Pastors in America?* 2007, www.churchleadership.org/apps/articles/default.asp?articleid=42347&columnid=4545, Accessed 08/06/2015.

[31] Deborah Beeksma, *The Average Christian Prays a Minute a Day; Prayer by the Faithful Helps Their Relationships,* GodDiscussion.com, 2013, Accessed 07/27/2015. Victory Life Church, VictoryLifeChurch.org, *Intercessory Prayer—Praying Always,* http://www.victorylifechurch.org/pdf/Intercessory_Praying_Always.pdf, Accessed 08/19/2015.

[32] Richard J. Krejcir, *Statistics on Pastors: What is Going on with the Pastors in America?* 2007, www.churchleadership.org/apps/articles/default.asp?articleid=42347&columnid=4545, Accessed 08/06/2015.

- 20% of Christians say they rarely or never pray for the spiritual status of others.[33]
- 42% of Christians say they find it difficult to find time on a regular, disciplined basis to pray and read the Bible.[34]
- 18% of Christians say they don't have a fixed pattern of prayer, but only pray when the chance or need arises.[35]
- 60% of Christians pray on the go.[36]
- Only 26% of Christians feel they have been equipped by their church to share their faith with others.[37]
- Numerous studies show that self-identified Christians are living lives indistinguishable from non-Christians (Jim Houston).[38]
- Only half of Christians believe in absolute moral truth (Barna).[39]
- 5% of Evangelical Protestants are living with their partner outside of marriage.[40]
- 14% of Evangelical Protestants are divorced or separated.[41]
- 39% of Protestant pastors believe it's okay to get a divorce if a

---

[33] Jon D. Wilke, *Churchgoers Believe in Sharing Faith, Most Never Do,* 2012, Lifeway.com, LifeWay Research, http://www.lifeway.com/Article/research-survey-sharing-christ-2012, Accessed 08/19/2015.

[34] Cath Martin, Evangelicals Admit Struggling to Find Time for Daily Bible Reading and Prayer, 2014, Christianity Today, www.christiantoday.com/article/daily.bible.reading.and.prayer.is.a.struggle.for.aany.evangelicals/36765.htm, Accessed 08/18/2015.

[35] Ibid., Accessed 08/19/2015.

[36] Ibid., Accessed 08/19/2015.

[37] Ibid., Accessed 08/19/2015.

[38] C. S. Lewis Institute, *Sparking a Discipleship Movement in America and Beyond,* cslewisinstitute.org, http://www.cslewisinstitute.org/webfm_send/210, Accessed 08/19/2015.

[39] Ibid., Accessed 08/19/2015.

[40] Pew Research Center, *Evangelical Protestant,* Pewforum.org, http://www.pewforum.org/religious-landscape-study/religious-tradition/evangelical-protestant, Accessed 08/19/2015.

[41] Ibid., Accessed 08/19/2015.

couple no longer loves one another.[42]

- Church discipline, an intensive form of discipleship for believers involved in serious sin, is virtually non-existent.[43]
- Churches today are often growing without depth (John Stott).[44]

Now to be fair, some of these stats fluctuate between various studies, but if they are even remotely accurate, the problem is still alarming. The stats reveal that the spiritual state, as a whole, of Evangelical churches and Christians in the Western world today is very troublesome and distant from what God intended. Michael Ramsden is disturbed about this and claims, "The American church is dying, not from the lack of evangelism, not from lack of resources, but from lack of effective discipleship."[45]

According to the stats, we're reaping damaging consequences for neglecting discipleship. As a result, most Christians are stuck in their growth in Christ and are failing to reach spiritual maturity. Dennis Hollinger cries out, "I'm convinced that what the world needs is not just more converts, but men and women who are authentic disciples of Christ, who love Christ with their whole being, and who will take their faith into the trenches of every sphere of life."[46]

Some things we can neglect and not adversely affect our spiritual health, but some things are foundational and critical to get right: understanding discipleship and the essential components of the discipleship-making process must be gotten

[42] LifeWay Research, *Views on Divorce Divide Americans,* 2015, LifeWayResearch.com, http://www.lifewayresearch.com/2015/08/12/views-on-divorce-divide-americans, Accessed 08/19/2015.
[43] R. Albert Mohler Jr, The Disappearance of Church Discipline–How Can We Recover? Part One, 2005, AlbertMohler.com, www.albertmohler.com/2005/05/13/the-disappearance-of-church-discipline-how-can-we-recover-part-one, Accessed 08/20/2015.
[44] C. S. Lewis Institute, *Sparking a Discipleship Movement in America and Beyond,* cslewisinstitute.org, http://www.cslewisinstitute.org/webfm_send/210, Accessed 08/19/2015.
[45] Ibid., Accessed 08/19/2015.
[46] Ibid., Accessed 08/19/2015.

right. Therefore, it's paramount we understand what's negatively affecting our commitment to discipleship. By neglecting discipleship, we reject God's nature and image, choosing instead to retain the image of sin and remain spiritually immature.

We can be certain that if the summation of Christ's and the Apostles' ministries was the command to make disciples, then Satan and his demonic cohort will do all they can to confuse and deter us in the process. We must not let them succeed!

Step 2: Measuring Your Overall Spiritual Maturity Level

Please put a mark (in pencil) to indicate what you think your present level of spiritual maturity is in each category.

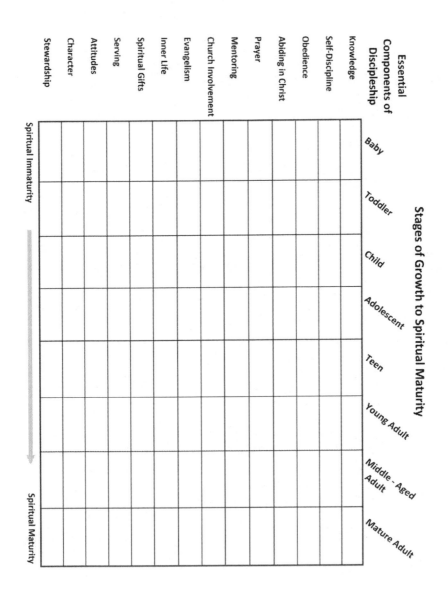

Step 3: Discussion Questions

1. Discuss the meaning of Matthew 28:16-20 that speaks of the Great Commission Mandate.

2. Discuss the meaning of Colossians 1:28–29 that speaks of the purpose for which the Apostles labored.

3. Discuss what you think your current overall level of spiritual maturity is (from the previous diagram) and why you feel you're at this level.

4. Discuss the priority Christ and the Apostles gave to discipleship and the priority the average church and Christian give it today.

5. Discuss the role discipleship plays in reaching spiritual maturity.

6. Discuss the warnings shared by modern day theologians and scholars regarding the neglect of discipleship today.

7. Discuss the consequences of neglecting discipleship according to the statistics.

8. Discuss your goals for growing in spiritual maturity as a result of participating in this book study.

Week 2: Knowledge of God and Discipleship

Step 1: Preliminary Reading

Of all the essential components for discipleship, none is as important as the knowledge of God. While the others are critical, I believe this component rises above them all. Donald Whitney states, "No spiritual discipline is more important than the intake of God's Word. Nothing can substitute for it. There is simply no healthy Christian life apart from a diet of the milk and meat of Scripture."[47]

Why Is God's Word So Vital to Discipleship?

God's Word forms the foundation upon which all the other essential components rest. It's the main component God uses in the transformation of our mind, which in turn, leads to spiritual maturity. Alister McGrath, in his article "The Passionate Intellect: Christian Faith and the Discipleship of the Mind," centers his focus of discipleship on the importance of knowledge.[48] He claims that theology was once the "queen of the sciences" and held in the highest esteem, but is no longer the case. It has declined in recent decades, and this should give us pause.[49]

McGrath believes knowledge serves believers in both their own personal understanding of God and in providing greater

---

[47] Donald Whitney, *Spiritual Disciplines for the Christian Life* (Colorado Springs: NavPress, 1991), p. 24.
[48] Alister McGrath, "The Passionate Intellect; Christian Faith and the Discipleship of the Mind" (Source: Pro Ecclesia, 22 no 1 Winter 2013, pp. 118-121. Publication Type: Review ATLA Religion Database with ATLASerials. Hunter Resource Library), Accessed 11/5/2014.
[49] Ibid., p. 118.

effectiveness in sharing this understanding with others. McGrath adds, "Christians need to realize that there is an intellectual core to the Christian faith which requires a discipleship of the mind in order to understand."[50] He further states, "Christians should be guided by a rational faith which provides the foundation for all their understanding of God and life."[51]

We Are Commanded to Love the Lord with Our Minds

The greatest command is to "Love the Lord your God with all your heart and with all your soul and **with all your mind** and with all your strength" (Mark 12:30). God wants us to love Him, not only with our heart, soul, and strength, but with our mind as well. A strong case can be made that loving God begins with loving Him with our minds because it's through our knowledge of Him that we understand how to love Him with our hearts. However, many are ignorant of this truth and are biblically illiterate.

We've noted that the latest Bible reading statistics of Christians, according to LifeWay Publishing, are dismal at best. Only 19% of Christians read their Bibles regularly. That leaves 81% of Christians who are basically biblically illiterate. These believers are certainly not loving God with their minds.

Christians Today and Biblical Illiteracy

Albert Mohler shares his concern about the state of evangelicalism and biblical illiteracy by asserting: "While America's Evangelical Christians are rightly concerned about the secular worldview's rejection of biblical Christianity, we ought to give some urgent attention to a problem much closer to home — biblical illiteracy in the church. This scandalous problem is our

---

[50] Ibid., p. 119.
[51] Ibid., p. 119.

own, and it's up to us to fix it."[52]

Researchers George Gallup and Jim Castelli state the problem bluntly, "Americans revere the Bible—but, by and large, they don't read it. And because they don't read it, they have become a nation of biblical illiterates. How bad is it? Researchers tell us that it's worse than most could imagine."[53]

The fact that the majority of so-called "Evangelical believers" rarely or never read their Bibles is staggering. It's no wonder many Christians today are "throwing in" with the new progressive morals of our culture and are spiritually immature.

Christians Today and Theological Illiteracy

Not only are many believers biblically illiterate, but they are theologically illiterate as well. They don't read theological books that would significantly deepen their knowledge of God and give them a correct worldview.

God has given gifted men and women to the church who have spent countless hours studying and writing books to aid us in becoming spiritually mature. However, only about 3% of believers read theological books and only about 10% read Christian, non-fiction books. Unfortunately, most Christians are indifferent and disregard these precious gifts of God, and as a result, choose to remain spiritually immature.

All the Components of Discipleship Rest upon God's Word

Every aspect of discipleship is linked to the knowledge of God's Word. Without it, we wouldn't know who God is, who we are, who others are, the purpose for our existence, the purpose for creation, where we have come from, where we are going, what God desires from us, and how we should behave. Some downplay

---

[52] Albert Mohler, *The Scandal of Biblical Illiteracy: It's Our Problem,* Christianity.com, http://www.christianity.com/1270946, Accessed 08/18/2015.
[53] Ibid., Accessed 08/18/2015.

the importance of the knowledge of Scripture, but in so doing, contradict the value Christ gives it.

During Christ's day, discipleship had a heavy focus on the knowledge of the Bible. Most disciples had much, if not the majority, of the Old Testament, memorized. They would go on discipleship training trips to get away from the distractions of life and focus on learning Scripture from their rabbi.

Christ placed enormous weight upon knowing Scripture and emphasized it throughout His ministry. In fact, Scripture is so important to God that He calls Christ the "Word." "In the beginning was the Word, and the Word was with God, and the Word was God . . . And the Word was made flesh, and dwelt among us" (John 1:1, 14). Christ is the Living Word! To say that the knowledge of Scripture is not important is to say that Christ is not important.

Klaus Issler, in his article "Six Themes to Guide Spiritual Formation Ministry Based on Jesus' Sermon on the Mount," makes the knowledge of God's Word one of his six major themes of discipleship. He states that it was important for Jesus' disciples to know Scripture, and interpret it correctly, to be able to follow its genuine teaching.[54] He goes on to say, "Jesus' own life was bathed in Scripture since the phrase 'It is written' or some variation occurs 23 times on his lips."[55]

How Can We Know God?

There are two basic ways to know God: (1) by observing His creation and (2) by knowing His Word. Theologically, we call the field of knowing God through His creation "General Revelation." All rational humans can know general things about God through

---

[54] Klaus Issler, "Six Themes to Guide Spiritual Formation Ministry Based on Jesus' Sermon on the Mount" (Source: Christian Education, Journal Date: September 1, 2010. CEJ: Series 3, Vol. 7, No. 2. ATLA Religion Database with ATLASerials. Hunter Resource Library), p. 372, Accessed 11/5/2014.

[55] Ibid., p. 372.

contemplating His creation: "For what can be **known about God** is plain to them, because God has shown it to them. For his **invisible attributes**, namely, **his eternal power** and **divine nature**, have been **clearly perceived**, ever since the creation of the world, in the things that have been made. So they are without excuse" (Rom. 1:19–20).

Through creation, every person knows certain truths about God. They know He is all-powerful, eternal, and all-knowing. Scripture also records in Psalm 19 that "The heavens declare the glory of God, and the sky above proclaims his handiwork. Day to day pours out speech, and night to night reveals knowledge. There is no speech, nor are there words, whose voice is not heard. Their voice goes out through all the earth, and their words to the end of the world" (Ps. 19:1–4). We see, then, that through creation all mankind has been blessed to know certain things about God.

While what we can know about God through His creation is amazing, it is nonetheless, limited. We don't know the details about God, just the big picture. How can we know the details? Through learning and applying God's Word to our lives. Theologically, we call the field of knowing God through His Word, "Special Revelation."

It's special because it's unique and allows us to know God in His fullness. It also gives us understanding about who we are, the purpose for life, the plan of God for His creation, and our surroundings — all extremely important things to know.

In the remainder of this section, we'll look at why knowing and applying God's Word to our lives is so essential to the discipleship-making process.

The Bible Is Unique and Unlike Any Other Writing Known to Mankind

- **The Bible claims to be inspired and to contain the very words of God:** 2 Timothy 3:16–17 states, "All Scripture is breathed out by God and profitable for teaching, for reproof, for correction, and for training in righteousness, that the man of God may be competent, equipped for every good work." Also, 2 Peter 1:20–21 affirms, "Knowing this first of all, that no prophecy of Scripture comes from someone's own interpretation. For no prophecy was ever produced by the will of man, but men spoke from God as they were carried along by the Holy Spirit." Unlike any other writing known to mankind, Scripture claims to be the very words of God.

- **The Bible claims to be living**: Hebrews 4:12 asserts, "For the word of God is living and active, sharper than any two-edged sword, piercing to the division of soul and of spirit, of joints and of marrow, and discerning the thoughts and intentions of the heart." Scripture is living and active because God inhabits His Word and speaks through it. No other writing is like it.

- **Christ affirmed the Bible to be the very Word of God**: Christ continually made statements concerning Scripture, such as "It is written," "So that the Scripture might be fulfilled," and "Have you not read?" He also used it continuously in His ministry and teaching. "And he said to them, 'O foolish ones, and slow of heart to believe all that the prophets have spoken! Was it not necessary that the Christ should suffer these things and enter into his glory?' And beginning with Moses and all the Prophets, he interpreted to them in all the Scriptures the things concerning himself" (Luke 24:25–27).

- **Christ claimed to be the very Word of God**: John 1:1 boldly states, "In the beginning was the Word, and the Word was with God, and the Word was God." Then John clarifies Who the Word is: "The **Word became flesh and dwelt among us**, and we have seen his glory, glory as of the only Son from the Father, full of grace and truth" (John 1:14). Not only do we have the written Word of God that claims to be living, but this living Word also is a Person called Jesus Christ.

- **The Apostles affirmed the Bible as the very Word of God**: The Apostles asserted that Scripture was inspired and used it continually. For example, Peter quoted large passages of Scripture in his sermon on the day of Pentecost, as found in Acts 2:14–42; quoting Joel 2:28–32, Psalm 16:8–11, and Psalm 110:1. The other Apostles also used a heavy dose of Scripture in their ministries.

- **The New Testament writers affirmed the Bible as the very Word of God:** God fashioned the New Testament to rest upon the foundation of the Old Testament. Therefore, God inspired the human writers of the New Testament to quote the Old Testament an amazing 855 times.[56] Many of these quotes were by Christ Himself, which gives further validation that Scripture is inspired and is the very Word of God.

- **History supports the Bible as being the Word of God:** The Bible has been the most important writing in the history of mankind. From its inception until the present, it has been the most read, the most valued, the most copied, the most discussed, the most quoted, and the most sold piece of literature ever. It has ranked far above all other writings. Moreover, countless millions of people claim it has changed their lives and have been willing to die for it.

- **The Bible claims to be eternal:** The Prophet Isaiah wrote, "The grass withers, the flower fades, but the word of our God will stand forever" (Isa. 40:8). The Apostle Peter penned, "But the word of the Lord remains forever. And this word is the good news that was preached to you" (1 Pet. 1:25). Moreover, Christ proclaimed, "Heaven and earth will pass away, but my

---

[56] Blue Letter Bible, BlueLetterBible.org, *Study Resources: Charts and Quotes,* www.blueletterbible.org/study/pnt/pnt08.cfm, Accessed 10/14/2015.

words will not pass away" (Matt. 24:35).

We Follow Christ by Following His Word

When Christ says, "Follow Me," He is telling us to follow Him and His commands. The original disciples entered into 3 ½ years of intense discipleship training with Christ, and then, after His death, His Spirit was with them as they continued as His disciples. Today, Christ primarily teaches us through His Word. However, the average believer spends little time learning from Christ through His Word. Therefore, they are unable to follow Christ.

Here's the latest Bible reading statistics of Christians according to LifeWay Publishing:[57]

- 19% read their Bibles daily or regularly
- 26% read their Bibles a few times a week
- 14% read their Bibles once a week
- 22% read their Bibles once a month
- 18% rarely or never read their Bibles

According to these stats, 81% of Christians don't read their Bibles regularly. That's unbelievable! And of the 19% who do read their Bibles regularly, many don't study or read it in-depth. Moreover, most don't read all of the Bible, but just parts of it as devotional reading.

In general, most Christians are eons away from being the kind of disciples who know and handle God's Word with precision and clarity as commanded in 2 Timothy 2:15. As a result, most Christians are babies or adolescents in their spiritual maturity, and are not serious about discipleship and becoming like Christ (Heb. 5:11–14). This is a severe indictment on the state

---

[57] Russ Rankin, *Study: Bible Engagement in Churchgoer's Hearts, Not Always Practiced,* Nashville, 2012, http://www.lifeway.com/Article/research-survey-bible-engagement-churchgoers, Accessed 07/23/2015.

of Christianity and discipleship today.

If the main avenue Christ used to teach His disciples was His words, and if the main avenue today is His words as found in Scripture, then most Christians today are extremely deficient in their ability to be disciples because their knowledge of Scripture is so desperately lacking. Unlike the original disciples who had much of Scripture committed to memory, many Christians today are biblically illiterate. Discipleship without a high dose of God's Word is impossible, as it's the main way Christ teaches us.

Following Christ means following His commands in Scripture. However, if we don't know His Word, we won't know His commands, so we'll be weak, ineffective disciples. We'll be disciples who grieve Christ instead of please Him.

God Expects Us to Know His Word

God instructs us in 2 Timothy 2:15 (NASB) to "Be **diligent** to present yourself **approved** to God as a workman who does not need to be ashamed, **accurately handling the word of truth**." God expects us to exert diligent effort in understanding and handling His Word, not to be indifferent and mediocre with it. 2 Peter 1:5 adds, "For this very reason, **make every effort** to supplement your faith with virtue, and virtue with **knowledge**." God commands us to know His Word, handle it correctly, and grow in it. In order to do this, we must be diligent and make every effort to know it.

The Importance of God's Word in Discipleship

As mentioned, Scripture is the most important component in the discipleship-making process because God supernaturally uses His inspired, living words to transform us into His image and bring us to full maturity in Christ.

The following are vital functions God's Word plays in discipleship and our growth in Christ:

- **It's food for our souls:** Matthew 4:2–4 asserts, "And after fasting forty days and forty nights, he was hungry. And the tempter came and said to him, 'If you are the Son of God, command these stones to become loaves of bread.' But he answered, 'It is written, Man shall not live by bread alone, but by every word that comes from the mouth of God.'" Scripture is the food that feeds our souls. In the same way our body hungers, the soul of a born-again believer hungers as well. Unfortunately, according to the Bible reading stats, 81% of believers are starving their souls, and by doing so, will never reach spiritual maturity.

- **It causes us to grow in Christ:** "But grow in the grace and knowledge of our Lord and Savior Jesus Christ" (2 Pet. 3:18). 1 Peter 2:2 adds, "Like newborn infants, long for the pure spiritual milk, that by it you may grow up into salvation—if indeed you have tasted that the Lord is good." Newborn infants have nothing on their mind except milk. We too, like newborn infants, should crave the Word of God so we can grow to spiritual maturity.

- **It renews our minds and changes our thinking:** Unlike any other writing known to mankind, Scripture transforms and renews our mind, which in turn, changes our behavior and brings us to spiritual maturity. Romans 12:2 declares, "Do not be conformed to this world, but be transformed by the renewal of your mind, that by testing you may discern what is the will of God, what is good and acceptable and perfect."

- **It strengthens our faith:** "So faith comes from hearing, and hearing through the word of Christ" (Rom. 10:17).

- **It gives us life:** "It is the Spirit who gives life; the flesh is no help at all. The words that I have spoken to you are spirit and life" (John 6:63). Also, Psalm 19:8 beautifully adds, "The precepts of the Lord are right, rejoicing the heart; the commandment of the Lord is pure, enlightening the eyes."

- **It instructs us in all matters:** "All Scripture is breathed out by God and profitable for teaching, for reproof, for correction, and for training in righteousness, that the man of God may be complete, equipped for every good work" (2 Tim. 3:16–17). Moreover, Psalm 119:105 states, "Your word is a lamp to my feet and a light to my path."

- **It protects us from sin and destruction:** King David attested, "I have stored up your word in my heart, that I might not sin against you" (Psalm 119:11).

- **It brings success in life:** God commanded Joshua to keep Scripture in the forefront of his life and meditate on it always so he would be successful: "This Book of the Law shall not depart from your mouth, but you shall meditate on it day and night, so that you may be careful to do according to all that is written in it. For then you will make **your way prosperous**, and then you will have **good success**" (Josh. 1:8).

Bible Intake

The role of Scripture in the life of a believer cannot be overemphasized. There are four key methods for acquiring it: (1) through reading, (2) through hearing, (3) through study, and (4) through memorization. The first three methods are the most common, and the last method, the least.

It's debatable as to whether or not Scripture memorization should be a separate and distinct essential component of the discipleship-making process as it has strong biblical and historical support. However, because it's part of the way we obtain the knowledge of God, I've included it in this category instead.

Personally, I've made Scripture memorization a part of my life and have experienced amazing benefits and blessings as a result. Not only has it sharpened my mental capabilities, but most of all, it has embedded the Word of God in my heart. I can say from experience that there's nothing like memorizing and meditating on God's Word. It's so rich, so powerful, so sweet, and so very life changing.

Conclusion

Bible intake is critical for attaining spiritual maturity and should not be neglected. To the degree we allow it to dwell in us richly and transform us will be the degree to which we will reach spiritual maturity. To the degree we neglect it will be the degree to which we will remain stunted and retarded in our spiritual growth.

Step 2: Measuring Your Level of Spiritual Maturity in the Knowledge of God

Self-Assessment Test for the Knowledge of God

Please take a moment to answer the following 10 questions to discover your spiritual maturity level regarding your knowledge of God. Answer each question using the following response options. Mark down your points earned for each question and then tally them up at the end to see your level of spiritual maturity in this category. As you take the test, avoid rushing. Answer the questions prayerfully and honestly. After you've taken the test, you might ask a loved one to take it for you as well. This will give you a broader perspective.

Points Possible per Answer

Never...................... 0 Points
Rarely .... 2 Points
Occasionally .... 4 Points
Frequently.............. 6 Points
Almost Always ...... 8 Points
Habitually.............. 10 Points

1. I read the entire Bible at least once every year. _____

2. I memorize Scripture regularly. _____

3. I have a daily quiet time with God. _____

4. I study the Bible. _____

5. I read the Bible daily. _____

6. I can give a detailed overview of the Bible. _____

7. I know the overview of each book of the Bible. _____

8. I know and can defend the major doctrines of the Bible with clarity and precision. _____

9. I read Christian non-fiction books. _____

10. I read theological books. _____

Total Score _____

Now check your score against the following chart to determine your spiritual maturity level for the knowledge of God.

Spiritual Maturity Grade from the "Knowledge" Test

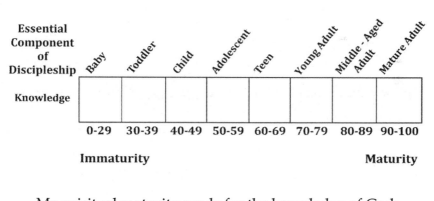

My spiritual maturity grade for the knowledge of God:

I am a _____ spiritually.

Step 3: Discussion Questions

1. Discuss the meaning of Hosea 6:6 that speaks of God's desire for us to know and obey Him instead of our tendency to take for granted and abuse His forgiveness and grace.

2. Discuss the meaning of 2 Peter 3:18 that speaks of God's desire for us to grow in our knowledge of Him.

3. Discuss your level of spiritual maturity in the knowledge of God and why you're at this level.

4. Discuss why God's Word is the most important component in the discipleship process.

5. Discuss the reason why so many Christians are biblically and theologically illiterate today.

6. Discuss the ways God's Word is unique and unlike any other writing known to mankind.

7. Discuss how in order to follow Christ we need to know His Word.

8. Discuss which of the following ideas in step 4 you plan on putting into practice and the goals you hope to achieve.

Step 4: Ideas for Growing in Your Knowledge of God

1. Establish a Bible reading plan for reading the entire Bible every year. You might consider the following options:

   - Reading the Bible chronologically.
   - Reading the Bible from beginning to end.
   - Dividing the Bible into three sections (Genesis–Psalms, Proverbs–Malachi, and Matthew–Revelation). Then read a chapter consecutively from each section daily.
   - Reading two chapters daily from the Old Testament and one chapter daily from the New Testament.
   - Reading the Old Testament once in a year and the New Testament twice in a year.

2. Start a Bible memorization plan. You can memorize selected verses, passages, chapters, and even entire books. It works great to get a 3x5 card, write your verse(s) down, and carry it with you. It's handy this way for memorization. You'll be surprised how much Scripture you can memorize in a year by just memorizing a verse or two a week.

3. Read all the introductions to the books of the Bible in a Study Bible, on the Internet, or from other sources. This will rapidly give you an overview of the whole Bible.

4. Do a Bible study on the knowledge of God.

5. Read an Old Testament survey book. This will give you an overview of the entire Old Testament.

6. Read a New Testament survey book. This will give you an overview of the entire New Testament.

7. Read a solid, lengthy, systematic theology work. Systematic theology takes each major doctrine of the Bible and looks at all the verses that deal with that doctrine. It's indispensable for understanding the major doctrines of the faith. It's good to

read several different systematic theology books to get a balanced view. Here are some suggestions:

- Wayne Grudem's *Systematic Theology*
- Charles Hodge's *Systematic Theology*
- Louis Berkhof's *Systematic Theology*
- Lewis Sperry Chafer's *Systematic Theology*
- Gordon Lewis and Bruce Demarest's *Integrative Theology*
- Millard Erickson's *Christian Theology*
- Charles Ryrie's *Basic Theology*
- Henry Thiessen's *Systematic Theology*

8. Read Old and New Testament theology works. These will aid you in understanding the big message and theme of both the Old and New Testaments (these are different from Old and New Testament survey books mentioned above).
9. Join an in-depth Bible study or start one of your own.
10. Read several books on how to correctly interpret the Bible (hermeneutics).
11. Take online Bible classes or even consider seeking an online Bible degree. There are many options available today, and some are even free.
12. Purchase a good Study Bible, and read the introductions and commentaries it offers.
13. Listen to Bible college lectures. Many Bible colleges now have many of their Bible class lectures online and are free. Great options are Biola/Talbot Bible College and Seminary, and Dallas Theological Seminary. Their lectures can be accessed via YouTube or iTunes.
14. Read other theological books.
15. Read Christian, non-fiction books.
16. Look for someone in your church who is deeply knowledgeable in God's Word and theology and ask him or her to mentor you in this area.

Week 3: Self-Discipline and Discipleship

Step 1: Preliminary Reading

Why is self-discipline so important that it's listed as an essential component of the discipleship-making process? Because it provides the structure, motivation, and perseverance necessary for attaining spiritual maturity, and the lack of it has been the downfall of countless Christians.

A strong case can be made that self-discipline is the most important factor needed for discipleship, and for that matter, life in general. Without it, none of the essential components of discipleship will be implemented and put into practice. Therefore, it can be argued that everything rests on discipline and without it, little else matters!

Donald Whitney boldly states, "I can say that I've never known a man or woman who came to spiritual maturity except through discipline. Godliness comes through discipline."[58] I believe Whitney is right. However, statistics today reveal that the average Christian has a definite lack of self-discipline. Due to this lack, many Christians are stuck in their journey toward spiritual maturity, and some will never arrive.

Discipleship Requires Self-Discipline

The word "disciple" is related to the word "discipline." A disciple, therefore, should be a highly disciplined person in following Christ. Without it, they will struggle.

As a pastor and missionary, I've seen firsthand the

---

[58] Donald Whitney, *Spiritual Disciplines for the Christian Life,* (Colorado Springs: NavPress, 1991), p. 15.

consequences the lack of self-discipline produces. I've seen people destroy their marriages, families, jobs, finances, health, bodies, and lives. I've seen countless people, who have wonderful hearts, live in pain and sorrow. Moreover, I've seen many Christians fail to reach spiritual maturity because they lack the self-discipline to attain it.

Self-Discipline Is a Key Purpose of the Book of Proverbs

Discipline is stated as a major theme of the Book of Proverbs: "For attaining wisdom and **discipline**; for understanding words of insight" (Prov. 1:2, NIV 1984).

A variant of the word "discipline" is mentioned 12 times throughout Proverbs, and the lack of discipline is mentioned numerous times: "And at the end of your life you groan, when your flesh and body are consumed, and you say, 'How I hated **discipline**, and my heart despised reproof!'" (Prov. 5:11–12).

Self-Discipline Is One of the Fruits of the Spirit

Galatians 5:23 states that self-control is a fruit that the Holy Spirit produces in the life of a believer. Self-control is synonymous with self-discipline. A self-controlled person is a disciplined person who makes themself do what they ought to do, not what they want to do.

Self-Discipline Is Related to Training

1 Timothy 4:6–8 uses the theme of training to convey the need for discipline in the Christian life: "If you put these things before the brothers, you will be a good servant of Christ Jesus, being **trained** in the words of the faith and of the good doctrine that you have followed. Have nothing to do with irreverent, silly myths. Rather **train yourself for godliness**; for while bodily training is of some value, godliness is of value in every way, as it holds promise for the present life and also for the life to come."

Here we see the value of discipline in training ourselves in godliness. However, most of us shy away from it. Bill Hull notes our tendency by stating, "Let's face it—discipline isn't something most of us like. We avoid discipline if we can, because it disrupts the normal and comfortable pattern of our life."[59]

Self-Discipline Is Related to Military Terminology

The Apostle Paul uses military vocabulary with Timothy in communicating the importance of self-discipline, enduring hardships, and being a tough soldier for Christ. He asserts, "Share in suffering as a good **soldier** of Christ Jesus" (2 Tim. 2:3). And again, "No **soldier** gets entangled in civilian pursuits, since his aim is to please the one who enlisted him" (2 Tim. 2:4).

According to the statistics of Christians today, self-discipline is lacking and needs to be built into our character if we're going to be deliberate disciples of Christ and reach spiritual maturity.

Self-Discipline Is Related to Sports Terminology

In 1 Corinthians 9:24–27, God uses sports language to convey the need for self-discipline:

Do you not know that in a race all the runners run, but only one gets the prize? Run in such a way as to get the prize. Everyone who competes in the games goes into **strict training**. They do it to get a crown that will not last, but we do it to get a crown that will last forever. Therefore, I do not run like someone running aimlessly; I do not fight like a boxer beating the air. No, I strike a blow to my body and make it my slave so that after I have preached to others; I

---

[59] Bill Hull, *The Complete Book of Discipleship: On Being and Making Followers of Christ* (The Navigators Reference Library 1, 2014, NavPress. Kindle Edition), Kindle Locations 445-447.

myself will not be disqualified for the prize.

The Apostle Paul uses the Olympic Games as a metaphor for the importance of discipline in our Christian lives. In the same way athletes competing in these games would undergo strict training, we too must submit ourselves to spiritual training in godliness in order to be faithful disciples.

The Role of Self-Discipline in Discipleship

In Joseph V. Crockett's article "Is There Discipline in Our Discipleship," he stresses that discipline is the major theme of discipleship. Crockett attests that "Even if you are an athlete, the term 'discipline' may not invoke warm and fuzzy feelings of excitement, yet discipline is necessary, even though it may not be welcomed."[60] Crockett challenges, "Where is the discipline in discipleship?"[61] Crockett even goes one step further and states that "It is difficult, if not impossible, to follow Jesus, to be His disciple, without accepting, embracing, and embodying spiritual disciplines for Christian formation."[62]

Raymond Edman also has strong words for us today: "We need the rugged strength of Christian character that can come only from discipline: the discipline of spirit, of mind, of body, of society."[63] Today, we are a soft, indulgent society! All our modern conveniences and luxuries have eaten away at our strength and discipline, and we're paying a high price for it.

Edman goes on to boldly state, "Discipleship means 'discipline!' The disciple is that one who has been taught or

---

[60] Joseph V. Crockett, "Is There Discipline in Our Discipleship?" (Source: Living Pulpit, Online, March 1, 2014, ATLA Religion Database with ATLASerials, Hunter Resource Library), p. 9, Accessed 11/5/2014.

[61] Ibid., p. 10.

[62] Ibid., p. 10.

[63] Raymond Edman, *The Disciplines of Life* (Minneapolis, Minnesota: World Wide Publications, 1948), preface.

trained by the Master, who has come with his ignorance, superstition, and sin, to find learning, truth, and forgiveness from the Savior. Without discipline, we are not disciples, even though we profess his name and pass for a follower of the lowly Nazarene."[64] Edman is so bold as to state that an undisciplined person is unable to be a disciple. These are strong words, words worth pondering and absorbing, words worth putting into practice!

Bill Hull sums up the thinking of many when he says, "Most of us want to reap the harvest of discipline while living a life of relative sloth."[65] Without self-discipline, we won't attain spiritual maturity or accomplish much for the Kingdom of God, and we'll arrive in heaven with few or no rewards.

The Importance of Spiritual Discipline

Developing spiritual discipline should be a high priority in our lives because it's the gasoline that powers spiritual growth. Without it, we'll stagnate and run aground. Therefore, we should purposefully make spiritual commitments despite how tough they might be. For example, every believer should establish the spiritual discipline to at least pray and read Scripture daily. Additional commitments can be made such as Bible memorization, journaling, spiritual gift development, reading, and fasting.

Establishing spiritual disciplines are biblical and have been used for millenniums. They take the theoretical and make it practical. They put "feet" on discipleship, applying it to where the rubber meets the road. We can say, "We should," or "It would be great if," but that gets us nowhere. Discipline is what moves us.

---

[64] Ibid., p. 9.
[65] Bill Hull, *The Complete Book of Discipleship: On Being and Making Followers of Christ* (The Navigators Reference Library 1, 2014, NavPress. Kindle Edition), Kindle Locations 451-452.

Spiritual disciplines establish clear, measurable, biblical steps that lead us to spiritual maturity. Christ practiced them, and they are found throughout Scripture. Donald Whitney states, "The Spiritual Disciplines are those personal and corporate disciplines that promote spiritual growth. They are the habits of devotion and experiential Christianity that have been practiced by the people of God since biblical times."[66] Whitney continues, "I will maintain that the only road to Christian maturity and godliness passes through the practice of the Spiritual Disciplines."[67]

Conclusion

Through self-discipline, we put into practice the principles that carry us to spiritual maturity. Without it, we remain spiritually immature. It provides the structure, motivation, and perseverance necessary for attaining spiritual maturity, and the lack of it has been the downfall of countless Christians.

A strong case can be made that self-discipline is the most important factor needed for discipleship, and for that matter, life in general. Without it, none of the essential components of discipleship will be implemented and put into practice. For this reason, it can be argued that everything rests on self-discipline and without it, little else matters!

[66] Donald Whitney, *Spiritual Disciplines for the Christian Life*, (Colorado Springs, NavPress, 1991), p. 15.
[67] Ibid., p. 14.

Step 2: Measuring Your Level of Spiritual Maturity in Self-Discipline

Self-Assessment Test for Self-Discipline

Please take a moment to answer the following 10 questions to discover your spiritual maturity level regarding self-discipline. Answer each question using the following response options. Mark down your points earned for each question and then tally them up at the end to see your level of spiritual maturity in this category. As you take the test, avoid rushing. Answer the questions prayerfully and honestly. After you've taken the test, you might ask a loved one to take it for you as well. This will give you a broader perspective.

Points Possible per Answer

Never...................... 0 Points
Rarely .... 2 Points
Occasionally .... 4 Points
Frequently............... 6 Points
Almost Always ...... 8 Points
Habitually............... 10 Points

1. I am a highly disciplined person. _____

2. I manage my time effectively. _____

3. I finish tasks I've started. _____

4. I bring every thought into obedience to Christ and His Word. _____

5. I stick to commitments without giving up. _____

6. I make myself do what I know I should do. _____

7. I put my responsibilities first and pleasures last. _____

8. I am a hardworking person. _____

9. I display godly attitudes despite how I feel. _____

10. I keep my inner heart and exterior surroundings extremely neat, clean, and organized. _____

Total Score _____

Now check your score against the following chart to determine your spiritual maturity level for self-discipline.

Spiritual Maturity Grade from the "Self-Discipline" Test

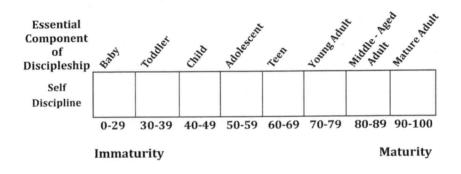

Essential Component of Discipleship	Baby	Toddler	Child	Adolescent	Teen	Young Adult	Middle-Aged Adult	Mature Adult
Self Discipline								
	0-29	30-39	40-49	50-59	60-69	70-79	80-89	90-100

Immaturity   Maturity

My spiritual maturity grade for self-discipline:

I am a _____ spiritually.

Step 3: Discussion Questions

1. Discuss the meaning of 1 Timothy 4:8.

2. Discuss the meaning of Hebrews 12:3–13.

3. Discuss your level of spiritual maturity in self-discipline and why you're at this level.

4. Discuss the role of self-discipline in the discipleship process and why it's so important.

5. Discuss the analogy of military and sports training in relation to the discipleship process.

6. Discuss ways in which we can develop more self-discipline in our lives.

7. Discuss the role of spiritual disciplines in relation to the discipleship process.

8. Discuss which of the following ideas in step 4 you plan on putting into practice and the goals you hope to achieve.

Step 4: Ideas for Growing in Self-Discipline

1. Acknowledge your weaknesses.
2. Pray and ask God for His grace and help.
3. Tell others about your goal to be more self-disciplined.
4. Read books and articles about self-discipline.
5. Memorize Scripture that deals with self-discipline (self-control).
6. Establish spiritual disciplines in your life that you do regularly such as:

   - Reading Scripture
   - Praying
   - Fasting
   - Memorizing Scripture
   - Reading non-fiction, Christian books
   - Giving
   - Serving

7. Remove unnecessary activities and distractions in your life.
8. Make yourself the boss of your body and will, not vice-versa.
9. Practice tolerating physical and emotional discomfort.
10. Visualize the long-term benefits of being self-disciplined.
11. Share your desire to be more disciplined with a loved one and ask them to hold you accountable for developing specific self-disciplines.
12. Set clear, measurable goals and deadlines.
13. Complete unfinished tasks.
14. Start an exercising program.
15. Establish routines in your life.
16. Acquire, or make, a self-discipline logbook and record the start and end times of your tasks and projects.
17. Replace bad habits with good ones.
18. Get up and go to bed at regular times.

19. Plan out your days, weeks, months, and years in advance.
20. Start the habit of using "To-do" lists to get things done and be more efficient in your life.
21. Clean up and organize your surroundings.
22. Reward yourself for your victories and accomplishments.
23. Penalize yourself when you fail.
24. Make a "Checklist Chart" of your commitments and check them off daily in order to build good habits in your life.
25. Find an accountability partner to hold you accountable for your goals.
26. Do a Bible study on self-discipline.
27. Look for someone in your church who is spiritually self-disciplined and ask him or her to mentor you in this area

Week 4: Obedience and Discipleship

Step 1: Preliminary Reading

The role of obedience is another vital component of discipleship. Without it, we go nowhere; with it, we go everywhere. The lack of obedience in the Christian life is one of the biggest roadblocks in our growth to spiritual maturity. Our choices are real and bring consequences in this life and the one to come. By obedience, we obtain God's richest blessings, and without it, we bring upon ourselves His discipline, displeasure, and judgment.

Christ's most used phrase, "Follow Me," calls for obedience, and it's impossible to follow Him without it. However, when 81% of Christians do not read their Bibles regularly, a whopping 61% of believers have not shared their faith in the last six months, 75% of church members do not attend a Bible study or small group, and the average Christian only prays somewhere between 1–7 minutes a day, it appears obvious that most Christians today are not obeying Christ as they should.

Obedience and Discipleship

Discipleship in the time of Christ called for strict adherence and obedience to a disciple's rabbi. No rabbi would even consider a candidate who was unwilling to pledge to him their total allegiance and obedience.

Christ employed this same concept in His call to discipleship: "And calling the crowd to him with his disciples, he said to them, 'If anyone would come after me, let him deny himself and take up his cross and follow me. For whoever would save his life will lose it, but whoever loses his life for my sake and the gospel's will save it'" (Mark 8:34–35). These verses call for obedience in the strictest manner. Christ knows that in order to follow Him, and be His disciple, we must have no other allegiance above Him. He calls for completely devoted followers.

Obedience and Legalism

Obedience is often viewed by many Christians as cold and opposed to God's love and grace. Some react to a focus on obedience as a form of legalism (the belief that our efforts earn salvation and God's love). It's true that obedience to a set of rules does not earn salvation or God's love, but it does please Him and is vitally necessary for growth in Christ. Without obedience, we displease God and grieve His Spirit (Eph. 4:30).

If we truly believe that the wages of sin is death, then we must acknowledge that obedience saves us from sin's destruction.

Interestingly, when God gave the Ten Commandments and the Mosaic Covenant on Mt. Sinai, obedience was the cornerstone component God required: "Now, therefore, if you will indeed **obey my voice and keep my covenant**, you shall be my treasured possession among all peoples, for all the earth is mine" (Ex. 19:5).

As mentioned, some within Christianity are uncomfortable with a focus on obedience as they see it as a form of legalism. However, what does Scripture teach? Is obedience opposed to God's love and grace? Interestingly, God says they are not. Consider the following verses:

- **John 14:15:** "If you love me, you will keep my commandments."

- **John 14:21:** "Whoever has my commandments and keeps them, he it is who loves me. And he who loves me will be loved by my Father, and I will love him and manifest myself to him."

- **John 15:10:** "If you keep my commandments, you will abide in my love, just as I have kept my Father's commandments and abide in his love."

- **John 15:14:** "You are my friends if you do what I command you."

- **1 John 2:3–4:** "And by this we know that we have come to know him, if we keep his commandments. Whoever says 'I know him' but does not keep his commandments is a liar, and the truth is not in him."

- **1 John 3:24:** "Whoever keeps his commandments abides in God, and God in him. And by this we know that he abides in us, by the Spirit whom he has given us."

- **Matthew 5:19:** "Therefore, whoever **relaxes one of the least of these commandments** and teaches others to do the same will be called least in the kingdom of heaven, but whoever does them and teaches them will be called great in the kingdom of heaven."

God makes it overwhelmingly clear that our love for Him (which is the greatest commandment) is expressed by our obedience. To not obey God is not to love Him! He asks for our obedience because He loves us and it's the best for us. Keeping His commandments is the greatest way we can love ourselves as they bring us life and blessings. God does not see obedience as legalism that is opposed to His love and grace but as the fulfillment and greatest expression of our love to Him.

Obedience and Knowing God

God says that the measuring stick for determining whether or not we actually "know" Him is through our obedience (1 John 2:3–4). Moreover, He says that obedience is the determining factor as to whether or not we are abiding in Him (1 John 3:24).

God expresses His love to us through His commands; we express our love to Him by obeying them.

Conclusion

The role of obedience is a critical component of discipleship. Without it, we go nowhere; with it, we go everywhere. The lack of obedience in the Christian life is one of the biggest roadblocks in our growth to spiritual maturity. God expects us to obey Him and is grieved when we don't. We show God how much we love Him through our obedience; we show Him our lack of love through our disobedience.

Obedience is a key factor in the discipleship process, and we'll get stuck in our spiritual growth if we don't take it seriously. If we presume upon God's love and grace, we greatly displease Him and damage ourselves in the process.

Step 2: Measuring Your Level of Spiritual Maturity in Obedience

Self-Assessment Test for Obedience to God

Please take a moment to answer the following 10 questions to discover your spiritual maturity level regarding your obedience to God. Answer each question using the following response options. Mark down your points earned for each question and then tally them up at the end to see your level of spiritual maturity in this category. As you take the test, avoid rushing. Answer the questions prayerfully and honestly. After you've taken the test, you might ask a loved one to take it for you as well. This will give you a broader perspective.

Points Possible per Answer

Never .... 0 Points
Rarely .... 2 Points
Occasionally .... 4 Points
Frequently.............. 6 Points
Almost Always ...... 8 Points
Habitually .... 10 Points

1. I read my Bible daily. _____

2. I walk close to God throughout the day. _____

3. I pray daily for at least 20 minutes. _____

4. I am deeply involved in a church. _____

5. I regularly share the gospel with others. _____

6. I am highly self-disciplined. _____

7. I maintain a clear conscience. _____

8. I have a ministry where I serve God and others. _____

9. I display excellent, Christ-like attitudes. _____

10. I manage my time, finances, and body, excellently. _____

Total Score _____

Now check your score against the following chart to determine your spiritual maturity level for obedience to God.

Spiritual Maturity Grade from the "Obedience" Test

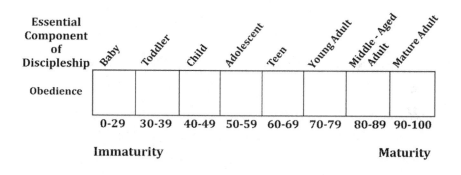

My spiritual maturity grade for obedience to God:

I am a _____ spiritually.

Step 3: Discussion Questions

1. Discuss the meaning of John 15:10.

2. Discuss the meaning of 1 John 2:3–5.

3. Discuss your level of spiritual maturity in obedience to God and why you're at this level.

4. Discuss the role of obedience in the discipleship process and why it's so important.

5. Discuss the relationship between legalism and obedience in the discipleship process.

6. Discuss how obeying God is related to knowing God.

7. Discuss how without obedience we can go nowhere in our Christian lives and will fail to reach spiritual maturity.

8. Discuss which of the following ideas in step 4 you plan on putting into practice and the goals you hope to achieve.

Step 4: Ideas for Growing in Obedience to God

1. Prayerfully ask yourself how obedient you are to God and His Word.
2. Ask loved ones and close friends to rate you in how obedient you are to God and His Word.
3. If you are not faithfully reading your Bible, begin now. Choose a Bible reading plan and make a commitment to obey God in this area (see ideas from the "Knowledge of God" section).
4. If you struggle in staying close to God throughout the day, consider setting your watch or smart phone to notify and remind you of God.
5. Put physical reminders up that remind you of God.
6. If you are struggling in obeying God in the area of prayer, commit to a set time and a set amount of time for prayer each day.
7. If you don't share the gospel much, look at the section in this chapter called "How to Grow in Evangelism" and study what the gospel is and how to share it. Then pray and look for opportunities to share your faith.
8. If you don't have a regular quiet time, make a commitment to do it faithfully each day.
9. If you don't give at least 10% of your income to the Lord's work, make a commitment to do so.
10. If you struggle in obedience in time management, finances, or taking care of your body, look at the section in this chapter called "How to Grow in Stewardship" and choose some ideas to help you be more obedient in these areas.
11. Prayerfully ask yourself if you allow Christ to control what you watch, read, hear, or think about, and commit to allowing

Him more control over what you're putting into your mind.

12. Read books and articles about how to obey God.
13. If you have broken relationships and need to ask forgiveness, or need to forgive someone, make a commitment to be obedient in this area.
14. If you are not serving God, make a commitment to get involved in some ministry within your church or community.
15. Do a Bible study on obedience.
16. Look for someone in your church who faithfully obeys God in all areas of their life and ask him or her to mentor you.

Week 5: Abiding in Christ and Discipleship

Step 1: Preliminary Reading

What does abiding in Christ mean and how does it play such a key role as one of the essential components of discipleship?

Christ gave a vivid illustration of what "abide" means and its importance in John 15:1-6:

> I am the true vine, and my Father is the vinedresser. Every branch in me that does not bear fruit he takes away, and every branch that does bear fruit he prunes, that it may bear more fruit. Already you are clean because of the word that I have spoken to you. **Abide** in me, and I in you. As the branch cannot bear fruit by itself, unless it **abides** in the vine, neither can you, unless you **abide** in me. I am the vine; you are the branches. Whoever **abides** in me and I in him, he it is that bears much fruit, for apart from me you can do nothing. If anyone does not **abide** in me he is thrown away like a branch and withers; and the branches are gathered, thrown into the fire, and burned.

Christ uses the word "abide" five times in this passage. The word "abide" means to remain in, or stay connected to something. One author has noted, "To abide is to live, continue, or remain— so to abide in Christ is to live in Him or remain in Him."[68]

John MacArthur defines abiding in Christ as "Remaining inseparably linked to Christ in all areas of life. We depend on Him for grace and power to obey. We look obediently to His Word for

---

[68] Gotquestions.org, *What Does It Mean to Abide in Christ?* http://www.gotquestions.org/abide-in-Christ.html, Accessed 10/20/2015.

instruction on how to live. We offer Him our deepest adoration and praise, and we submit ourselves to His authority over our lives. In short, Christians should gratefully know that Jesus Christ is the source and sustainer of their lives."[69]

Grapevines and Abiding in Christ

The illustration of the vine and the branches in John 15 provides an incredible picture of what abiding means. A branch is completely dependent upon the vine for its nutrients and life. The moment it's detached, it quickly withers and dies.

Many years ago, I managed a vineyard and saw this firsthand. Often, due to the wind, a tractor, or other reasons, a branch would get disconnected from its vine. Within minutes, the branch would begin withering and dying. Grapevines are very different from other plants and are more susceptible to withering than most. That's why Christ used this illustration. He knew the Jewish culture was familiar with grapevines and would instantly understand His point.

Therefore, in the same way a grape branch withers and dies if it is not connected to its vine, we as well, will wither and die spiritually if we don't stay connected to Christ and abide in Him.

Walking in the Spirit and Abiding in Christ

Abiding in Christ can also be defined as walking in the Spirit or being led by the Spirit. "But I say, walk by the Spirit, and you will not gratify the desires of the flesh. For the desires of the flesh are against the Spirit, and the desires of the Spirit are against the flesh, for these are opposed to each other, to keep you from doing the things you want to do. But if you are led by the Spirit, you are not under the law" (Gal. 5:16–18).

---

[69] John MacArthur, *What Does It Mean to "Abide" in Christ?* Gty.org, www.gty.org/resources/Questions/QA161/What-does-it-mean-to-abide-in-Christ, Accessed 10/20/2015.

Setting Our Minds on Christ and Abiding in Christ

Abiding in Christ means we are constantly setting our minds upon Him and His Word throughout our waking hours and seeking to obey Him. We take into consideration what He thinks, we pray for His help and guidance often, and we are in tune with His Spirit within us.

We don't wander far from Him throughout the day, are constantly checking in with Him, and are bringing every thought into obedience to Him and His Word (2 Cor. 10:4–5). We, in essence, live in the presence of God and pray without ceasing (1 Thess. 5:17). Praying without ceasing doesn't mean we do nothing else during the day but bow our heads in prayer; but rather, it carries the idea of living in the presence of God and attempting to please and obey Him in all things.

Seeking the Things Above and Abiding in Christ

Colossians 3:1–2 also helps us understand what the word "abide" means: "If then you have been raised with Christ, seek the things that are above, where Christ is, seated at the right hand of God. Set your minds on things that are above, not on things that are on earth." Abiding means we set our minds on God, on His Word, and on seeking His Kingdom. It values the things of God over the things of earth and continually makes adjustments that reflect this priority.

Conclusion

John 15:5 says, "Whoever abides in me and I in him, he it is that bears much fruit, for **apart from me you can do nothing**." Without abiding in Christ, we can do nothing. We cannot be disciples, we cannot have right attitudes, we cannot grow in Christ, we cannot attain spiritual maturity, and we are absolutely helpless and dead. This is why abiding in Christ is so important.

Step 2: Measuring Your Level of Spiritual Maturity in Abiding in Christ

Self-Assessment Test for Abiding in Christ

Please take a moment to answer the following 10 questions to discover your spiritual maturity level for abiding in Christ. Answer each question using the following response options. Mark down your points earned for each question and then tally them up at the end to see your level of spiritual maturity in this category. As you take the test, avoid rushing. Answer the questions prayerfully and honestly. After you've taken the test, you might ask a loved one to take it for you as well. This will give you a broader perspective.

Points Possible per Answer

Never.......................	0 Points
Rarely	2 Points
Occasionally	4 Points
Frequently..............	6 Points
Almost Always	8 Points
Habitually	10 Points

1. I have a daily quiet time with God.   _____

2. I seek earnestly to live in the presence of God.   _____

3. I pray to God throughout the day.   _____

4. I think of God throughout the day.   _____

5. I make all my decisions based upon God's Word.   _____

6. I bring every thought into obedience to Christ. _____

7. I display godly attitudes and character. _____

8. I live with eternity in mind. _____

9. I trust Christ and remain strong in trials and hardships. _____

10. I carefully listen for God's voice throughout the day. _____

Total Score _____

Now check your score against the following chart to determine your spiritual maturity level for abiding in Christ.

Spiritual Maturity Grade from the "Abiding in Christ" Test

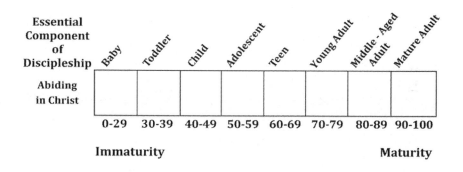

My spiritual maturity grade for abiding in Christ:

I am a _____ spiritually.

Step 3: Discussion Questions

1. Discuss the meaning of John 15:1–6.

2. Discuss the meaning of 2 John 1:9.

3. Discuss your level of spiritual maturity in abiding in Christ and why you're at this level.

4. Discuss the role of abiding in Christ in the discipleship process and why it's so important.

5. Discuss the illustration of grapevines and abiding in Christ.

6. Discuss how walking in the Spirit is related to abiding in Christ as found in Galatians 5:16–18.

7. Discuss what it means to practically seek "the things that are above" in relation to abiding in Christ and the discipleship process as found in Colossians 3:1–2.

8. Discuss which of the following ideas in step 4 you plan on putting into practice and the goals you hope to achieve.

Step 4: Ideas for Growing in Abiding in Christ

1. Start or be more faithful in a daily quiet time.
2. Consider some kind of reminder that causes you to check in with God throughout the day to be more in tune with Him. You might set a timer on your smartphone, put a picture somewhere, or establish a habit of praying and thinking about God more often. Daniel set aside a time to pray three times a day; maybe you might consider doing the same.
3. Seek an accountability partner to help you set your mind upon God more frequently.
4. Memorize Scripture that speaks of abiding in Christ (John 15:1–11; Col. 3:1–4; Ps. 1; Gal. 5:16–25).
5. Read books and articles on abiding in Christ.
6. Pray daily for God's help in learning how to abide in Him.
7. Saturate your mind more with Scripture, which will help greatly in causing you to think more about God.
8. Listen to Christian radio.
9. Listen to Christian music.
10. Listen to sermons on abiding in Christ.
11. Give up the activities in your life that are standing in the way of your full commitment to Christ.
12. Fast and pray to train yourself to abide in Christ better.
13. Reflect or journal on the activities of your day, thinking about how you used your time, how you walked with God, and what you could have done differently.
14. Do a Bible study on abiding in Christ.
15. Look for someone in your church who faithfully abides in Christ and ask him or her to mentor you in this area.

Week 6: Prayer and Discipleship

Step 1: Preliminary Reading

As we noted earlier, according to recent stats, the average Evangelical Christian prays between 1–7 minutes a day. In addition, Daniel Henderson did some recent research and discovered the following stats regarding Christians and prayer. He states the average person lives 77 years. That equates to 28,000 days, 670,000 hours, or 40 million minutes, and during their lifetime, they spend this time doing the following things:[70]

- The average person spends 24 minutes a day getting dressed. That equals 13 hours a month, 7 days a year, or 1 year in a lifetime.
- The average person spends 40 minutes a day on the phone. That factors out to 20 hours a month, 10 days a year, or 2 years in a lifetime.
- The average person spends 1 hour a day in the bathroom. That amounts to 30 hours a month, 15 days a year, and 3 years in a lifetime.
- The average person spends 3 hours a day watching television. That is 90 hours a month, 45 days a year, and 9 years in a lifetime.
- The average Christian spends less than 10 minutes a day in prayer. That equates to less than 6 hours a month, 3 days a year, and 7 months in a lifetime.[71]

What a tragedy that prayer, which should be our most

---

[70] Daniel Henderson, *No Time to Pray,* Praying Pastor Blog, PrayingPastorBlog.blogspot, http://prayingpastorblog.blogspot.mx/2009/02/no-time-to-pray-no-time-to-pray.html, Accessed 10/16/2015.
[71] Ibid., Accessed 10/16/2015.

important priority receives the least amount of time and attention. Christians have time to talk on the phone 40 minutes a day and watch TV 3 hours a day but can only pray less than 10 minutes a day. What's the problem? The only reasonable explanation is that it's not very important, and therefore, not a priority. Can you imagine how God feels about that? He's worth less than TV, phone time, the Internet, and almost every other activity!

Another recent survey shows even more disturbing news. It reveals that the average Christian prays just a minute a day: "It appears Christian prayers have apparently morphed into tweets to God."[72] Deborah Beeksma quotes the Rev. Nathan Shutes as saying, "My fear is that this generation has missed out on [being] prayer warriors. We have become an instant gratification generation. We tweet in 140 characters, and prayer can be just as short. Here are some numbers that ought to make you cringe; on the Baptist Board website, they say the average Christian prays a minute a day, and the average pastor prays five minutes a day. God have mercy on us for such little devotion to the Sovereign One of the universe. No wonder our nation is falling away from God."[73]

What Is Prayer?

Mary Fairchild suggests, "Prayer is not a mysterious practice reserved only for clergy and the religiously devout. Prayer is simply communicating with God — listening and talking to him. Believers can pray from the heart, freely, spontaneously, and in their own words."[74] Andrew Murray also enhances our understanding of prayer when he says, "Prayer is not monologue,

---

[72] Deborah Beeksma, *The Average Christian Prays a Minute a Day; Prayer by the Faithful Helps Their Relationships,* GodDiscussion.com, 2013, Accessed 07/27/2015.
[73] Ibid., Accessed 07/27/2015.
[74] Mary Fairchild, *Basics to Prayer,* Christianity.About.com,
http://christianity.about.com/od/prayersverses/a/basicstoprayer.htm, Accessed 10/16/2016.

but dialogue; God's voice is its most essential part. Listening to God's voice is the secret of the assurance that He will listen to mine."[75]

Through prayer, we can be honest, open, express our frustrations, problems, joys, and sorrows. Prayer is simple, yet its effects are powerful. Prayer connects us to the ultimate power of the universe because it connects us with the Sovereign, Almighty God, Ruler, Owner, and King of it. No time spent in prayer is wasted; on the contrary, there is nothing more important we could do.

The Importance of Prayer in Discipleship

We see the importance of prayer all throughout the Bible. It's mentioned around 316 times and was a key characteristic of all godly men and women. Richard Foster, in his book *Celebration of Discipline,* claims that prayer is one of the most important aspects of discipleship: "Of all the Spiritual Disciplines, prayer is the most central because it ushers us into perpetual communion with the Father."[76] Moreover, Foster says, "All who have walked with God have viewed prayer as the main business of their lives."[77]

Jesus and Prayer

Unlike the average Christian, who prays around 1–7 minutes a day, prayer throughout the Bible is seen as a central focus of life. Christ set an impeccable example in His prayer life despite being, in very essence, God:

- He prayed regularly and on many occasions got away by Himself to spend time with the Father.

[75] Andrew Murray, Power to Change, Great Quotes on Prayer, http://powertochange.com/experience/spiritual-growth/prayerquotes, Accessed 11/16/2015.
[76] Richard Foster, *Celebration of Discipline* (HarperCollins, Kindle Edition, 2009), p. 33.
[77] Ibid., p. 34.

- After feeding the 5,000 and dismissing the crowd, Scripture records, "He went up on the mountain by himself to pray. When evening came, he was there alone" (Matt. 14:23).

- Despite His busyness, He made time for prayer: "And rising very early in the morning, while it was still dark, he departed and went out to a desolate place, and there he prayed" (Mark 1:35).

- Before making the immeasurable decision to choose the twelve disciples, He spent a whole night in prayer to seek His Father's will: "In these days he went out to the mountain to pray, and all night he continued in prayer to God. And when day came, he called his disciples and chose from them twelve, whom he named apostles" (Luke 6:12–13).

- He stressed the importance of prayer to His disciples: "And he told them a parable to the effect that they ought always to pray and not lose heart" (Luke 18:1).

- Christ also overcame temptation and taught His disciples to do the same through prayer: "Watch and pray that you may not enter into temptation. The spirit indeed is willing, but the flesh is weak" (Matt. 26:41).

- We also find in John 17, the better part of an entire chapter, wherein Christ devoted Himself to prayer for His disciples and all who would follow Him afterward.

The Apostles and Prayer

Following Christ's example and teaching on the importance of prayer, the Apostles, and the early church also prayed constantly.

- Shortly after Christ's resurrection, the disciples continued in prayer: "All these with one accord were devoting themselves

71

to prayer, together with the women and Mary the mother of Jesus, and his brothers" (Acts 1:14).

- After the church was born on Pentecost, the early church devoted themselves to prayer: "And they devoted themselves to the apostles' teaching and the fellowship, to the breaking of bread and the prayers" (Acts 2:42).

- The lame man that Peter and John healed at the temple was a result of going to the temple to pray (Acts 3:1).

- After being persecuted for preaching the Word, the disciples, and the early church prayed for boldness to keep pressing on: "And when they had prayed, the place in which they were gathered together was shaken, and they were all filled with the Holy Spirit and continued to speak the word of God with boldness" (Acts 4:31).

- When faced with busyness and administrative challenges, prayer became a priority of the elders of the early church: "But we will devote ourselves to prayer and to the ministry of the word" (Acts 6:4).

- Prayer also accompanied each missionary journey by Paul and his companions: "Then after fasting and praying they laid their hands on them and sent them off" (Acts 13:3).

Christians Today and Prayer

The Bible is replete with examples of godly men and women praying. Yet today, the average Christian prays between 1–7 minutes a day. What a contrast! Samuel Chadwick states, "The one concern of the devil is to keep Christians from praying. He fears nothing from prayerless studies, prayerless work, and prayerless religion. He laughs at our toil, mocks at our wisdom, but he trembles when we pray."[78] It appears Satan is rejoicing over the lack of prayer in the lives of many Christians today.

Why should we pray, and why does it play such a large role in discipleship and our transformation towards spiritual maturity? Scripture provides, at least, six essential reasons:

1. By Prayer, We Have a Relationship with God

Having a relationship with the living God is the essence of the Christian life and our purpose for existing. It's what God sought to regain with mankind after their fall in the Garden of Eden and is a determining factor in whether a person is saved or not. The simple fact is that we cannot have a relationship with God without prayer. It's how we communicate and talk to Him.

Dan Hayes says it well, "I am first called to prayer because it is a key vehicle to building my love relationship with Jesus Christ. Hear me now — this is important. Christianity is not primarily rules. It is relationship."[79]

We are to love the Lord our God with all our heart, soul, mind, and strength. Christ exemplified this truth in His prayer life with the Father. He continually was in communion with the Father and walked every step while listening to His voice.

If we want to have a relationship with God, then we must pray. Samuel Chadwick states, "Prayer is the acid test of devotion."[80] It's in our obedience and commitment to commune with our Father that we show Him our true love.

2. By Prayer, God Gives Us the Power to Overcome Temptation

Christ provides compelling instruction, and an example, on

---

[78] Christian Prayer Quotes, *Prayer Quotations,* http://www.christian-prayer-quotes.christian-attorney.net, Accessed 10/20/2015.
[79] Dan Hayes, *Motivating Reasons to Pray,* StartingWithGod.com, www.startingwithgod.com/knowing-god/motivating, Accessed 10/20/2015.
[80] Christian Prayer Quotes, *Prayer Quotations,* http://www.christian-prayer-quotes.christian-attorney.net, Accessed 10/20/2015.

how to overcome temptation. In Luke 22:39–46, Christ is facing His last hours on earth before being crucified. He is in the Garden of Gethsemane, embracing the reality of paying for the sins of mankind for all time and eternity. He begins this time by teaching His disciples how to overcome temptation: "And he came out and went, as was his custom, to the Mount of Olives, and the disciples followed him. When he came to the place, he said to them, '**Pray that you may not enter into temptation.**'" Then Christ practiced what He taught: "And he withdrew from them about a stone's throw, and knelt down and prayed, saying, 'Father, if you are willing, remove this cup from me. Nevertheless, not my will, but yours, be done.'"

Christ's temptation to avoid the pain of the Cross was so intense that His sweat became bloody: "And being in an agony he prayed more earnestly; and his sweat became like great drops of blood falling down to the ground." Despite His temptation, He remained in prayer, yielded to God's will, and was victorious over the Cross and death.

Afterward, He returned to His disciples to find them half-asleep. He then told them again about prayer and its role in temptation: "And when he rose from prayer, he came to the disciples and found them sleeping for sorrow, and he said to them, 'Why are you sleeping? Rise and pray that you may not enter into temptation.'"

Interestingly, Christ began His instruction on how to overcome temptation by telling the disciples about prayer, then showing by example how to do it, and then repeating His instruction again.

If we're going to be victorious over temptation, we need to follow Christ's example. Unfortunately, much of the time, prayer is not the first thing we do when confronting temptation, so we succumb and fall as a result. How much better we would be if it were our first line of defense. Dan Hays asserts, "What about seeing prayer as our first option so that God can give us courage and strength prior to our temptations? Certainly, if we would pray more, we would yield less to sin!"[81]

3. By Prayer, God Leads and Directs Our Paths

There are two general areas in life where we need God's direction: (1) in fully understanding truth and morals already revealed in the Bible and (2) in the practical areas of life that Scripture does not address.

God has already revealed much of His will to us through Scripture. For example, His will is that we become saved, are transformed into the image of Christ, attain spiritual maturity, and that we love God and others. However, in matters not directly revealed in Scripture, it gets trickier. Areas like whom we should marry, what job we should take, or what college we should attend, become harder to discern.

If we obey God in the areas already revealed in Scripture, then the areas not revealed will become much simpler to perceive. However, if we are disobedient to God's clear, revealed will in Scripture, then we'll struggle to find His will in other matters as well.

It's also important to note that Scripture provides wisdom and direction for finding His will by directing us to others. Proverbs 11:14 speaks of the role of counselors, Proverbs 1:8 shows the role of our parents, and James 1:5 speaks of directly receiving wisdom from God through prayer.

Through prayer, God will miraculously open and close doors in our lives. He loves us dearly, and when He sees His children seeking His Kingdom first and desiring above all else to please Him, He goes out of His way to supernaturally guide and direct

---

[81] Dan Hays, *Motivating Reasons to Pray,* StartingWithGod.com, www.startingwithgod.com/knowing-god/motivating, Accessed 10/20/2015.

their paths.

4. By Prayer, We Accomplish God's Work

Charles Spurgeon declared, "I would rather teach one man to pray than ten men to preach."[82] Moreover, Andrew Murray claimed, "The man who mobilizes the Christian church to pray will make the greatest contribution to world evangelization in history."[83]

Prayer rallies the power of the Almighty and involves Him in our efforts. With Him, we are everything, but without Him, we are nothing. Christ said, "I am the vine; you are the branches. Whoever abides in me and I in him, he it is that bears much fruit, for **apart from me you can do nothing**" (John 15:5).

A careful look at Scripture reveals that everything accomplished for God happens through prayer. The births of Isaac, the Prophet Samuel, and John the Baptist all came through prayer. The wisdom of Solomon, the dedication of the temple, and the countless deliverances of Israel from her enemies came through prayer. The work of Christ, the works of the early church, and the spread of the gospel all came through prayer. Likewise, if we want God's blessing in our lives and ministries, it will only come through prayer as well.

5. By Prayer, We Are Victorious in Spiritual Warfare

The battle between good and evil and the reality of spiritual warfare is clear in Scripture. We see it in the life and ministry of Christ, the Apostles, and the early church. It is also specifically addressed in Ephesians 6:12: "For we do not wrestle against flesh and blood, but against the rulers, against the authorities, against the cosmic powers over this present darkness, against the spiritual

---

[82] Christian Prayer Quotes, *Prayer Quotations,* http://www.christian-prayer-quotes.christian-attorney.net, Accessed 10/20/2015.
[83] Ibid., Accessed 10/20/2015.

forces of evil in the heavenly places."

It's through prayer that we tap into God's power and become victorious over Satan and his evil forces. We are no match for them on our own, but we are more than conquerors over them through Christ.

Prayer is also the overarching armor in our spiritual warfare: "Praying at all times in the Spirit, with all prayer and supplication. To that end keep alert with all perseverance, making supplication for all the saints" (Eph. 6:17–18).

6. By Prayer, God Grants Us Peace

We find peace through prayer: "Casting all your anxieties on him, because he cares for you" (1 Pet. 5:7).

Additionally, "Do not be anxious about anything, but in everything by prayer and supplication with thanksgiving let your requests be made known to God. And the peace of God, which surpasses all understanding, will guard your hearts and your minds in Christ Jesus" (Phil. 4:6–7).

Prayer is what alleviates our worries and stress. It ushers God's peace into our hearts by taking our burdens, and concerns, and placing them on God.

Conclusion

By prayer, we have a relationship with God, overcome temptation, find God's will, accomplish much for God's Kingdom, are victorious in spiritual warfare, and receive God's peace. As the great prayer warrior E. M. Bounds says, "Prayer should not be regarded as a duty which must be performed, but rather as a privilege to be enjoyed, a rare delight that is always revealing some new beauty."[84] Prayer is an essential component of discipleship, and without it, spiritual maturity is unattainable.

---

[84] Ibid., Accessed 10/20/2015.

Step 2: Measuring Your Level of Spiritual Maturity in Prayer

Self-Assessment Test for Prayer

Please take a moment to answer the following 10 questions to discover your spiritual maturity level regarding prayer. Answer each question using the following response options. Mark down your points earned for each question and then tally them up at the end to see your level of spiritual maturity in this category. As you take the test, avoid rushing. Answer the questions prayerfully and honestly. After you've taken the test, you might ask a loved one to take it for you as well. This will give you a broader perspective.

Points Possible per Answer

Never .... 0 Points
Rarely .... 2 Points
Occasionally .... 4 Points
Frequently............... 6 Points
Almost Always ...... 8 Points
Habitually .... 10 Points

1. I have a designated prayer time daily. _____
2. I confess my sins and pray for forgiveness daily. _____
3. I maintain an attitude of prayer throughout the day. _____
4. I pray daily for at least 20 minutes. _____
5. I thank God for His blessings daily. _____

6. I pray for others daily.   _____

7. I pray for God's help to walk closely with Him daily. _____

8. I listen for God's voice during my prayer times.   _____

9. I pray with others for the needs of God's Kingdom. _____

10. I pray for my needs daily.   _____

Total Score   _____

Now check your score against the following chart to determine your spiritual maturity level for prayer.

Spiritual Maturity Grade from the "Prayer" Test

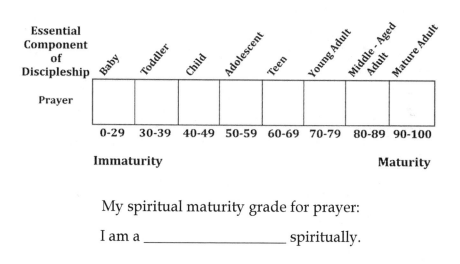

My spiritual maturity grade for prayer:

I am a _____ spiritually.

Step 3: Discussion Questions

1. Discuss the meaning of 1 Thessalonians 5:16–18.

2. Discuss the meaning of Colossians 4:2.

3. Discuss your level of spiritual maturity in prayer and why you're at this level.

4. Discuss the role of prayer in the discipleship process and why it's so important.

5. Discuss the role of prayer in the life of Christ.

6. Discuss the role of prayer in the life of the Apostles and early church.

7. Discuss the six purposes of prayer in relation to the discipleship process.

8. Discuss which of the following ideas in step 4 you plan on putting into practice and the goals you hope to achieve.

Step 4: Ideas for Growing in Prayer

1. Set aside a fixed time for daily prayer.
2. Make prayer a daily habit.
3. Set aside a fixed place for prayer that is free from distractions.
4. Establish prayer topics to help you during your prayer time. Here are some ideas to include:
   - Confess your sins to God and ask Him to reveal unknown sin in your life, or things that are displeasing to Him. This may include broken relationships, wrong activities, mismanagement of time, neglect of God, laziness, allowing sinful things into your mind, and apathy.
   - Pray for the filling of God's Spirit in your life.
   - Pray for help in walking with God and setting your mind on Him.
   - Thank God for all His blessings in your life.
   - Praise God for who He is and what He's done for you.
   - Pray for family members.
   - Pray for unsaved loved ones and friends.
   - Pray for missionaries, pastors, churches, Christian organizations, etc.
   - Pray for your own needs.
   - Pray for your ministry or ministries.
   - Pray for government leaders.
   - Pray for guidance and direction in your life.
   - Pray for opportunities to evangelize.
5. Consider doing a "prayer walk" around some ministry, church, neighborhood, or place that needs Christ.
6. Join your church's prayer team and pray for needs that arise.
7. Start a prayer meeting.
8. Start a prayer journal and keep track of your own prayer requests and those of others. Your faith will be strengthened

as you see God faithfully answer prayer.

9. Create a "prayer wall" and post your prayer requests on it.

10. Put prayer requests on your fridge.

11. Set aside meditative prayer times by going to the beach, going on a hike, going to a lake, or going for a walk.

12. Give up something this week to spend more time in prayer.

13. Make a commitment to fast and pray, setting aside a meal, or a full day.

14. Read books and articles on prayer.

15. Do a Bible study on prayer.

16. Look for someone in your church who faithfully prays and ask him or her to mentor you in this area.

Week 7: Mentoring and Discipleship

Step 1: Preliminary Reading

One of the central themes of discipleship during the time of Christ was that of relationships and mentoring. It was normal for a rabbi to take his disciples on trips that lasted from several days to several weeks in order to train them. They would dedicate this time for intense mentoring, teaching, practicing, and learning. All the distractions of life would be set aside for the purpose of interaction between the rabbi and his students. Teaching was highly relational and modeled, and the disciples would learn how to apply Scripture, in large part, by observing the conduct and practices of their rabbi.

What Is Mentoring?

Biblical mentoring is an informal relationship wherein a more spiritually mature person teaches and models godly, life-skills to others who are generally less spiritually mature. It can be formal, informal, take place in a group setting, take place in an individual setting, can be regular, or somewhat sporadic.

Examples of mentoring include small group Bible studies, Sunday School classes, youth group, one on one discipleship studies, accountability partners, and so forth.

The most effective mentoring takes place in a one on one setting, or in a small group where specific truths and life-skills are intentionally passed on.

Mentoring Provides an Example

Christ was a rabbi who modeled what He taught to His disciples. This was done as they spent time together, took trips together, lived together for periods of time, and served together. After learning from Christ, His disciples would then practice what they learned.

We see mentoring as a central focus for teaching and training in other examples from Scripture as well: Moses mentored Joshua, Naomi mentored Ruth, Elijah mentored Elisha, and Paul mentored Timothy. After Paul had mentored Timothy, he encouraged Timothy to mentor others: "You then, my child, be strengthened by the grace that is in Christ Jesus, and what you have heard from me in the presence of many witnesses entrust to faithful men who will be able to teach others also" (2 Tim. 2:2).

Modern-Day Discipleship

Discipleship in our day is very different from what it was in the time of Christ. Today, we primarily focus on teaching certain truths and think that after several classes on discipleship training we're finished. Normally, this is because we're focusing primarily on imparting knowledge and not on all the essential components of discipleship like character, attitudes, spiritual gift development, self-discipline, and so on.

Discipleship is much more than taking a class for several weeks and thinking we're done. Instead, it must be engaged in throughout our lifetime. We are never finished and must always be looking for new opportunities to grow in all the essential components of the discipleship-making process.

Mentoring in the Church

A number of recent scholars and theologians have highlighted the importance of mentoring in discipleship. Voddie Baucham Jr., in his article "Equipping the Generations: A Three-Pronged Approach to Discipleship," shows that Paul clearly instructs Titus to make disciples using a mentoring model.[85] There are three key themes Baucham draws out from the Book of Titus that underscores what successful discipleship should entail:

1. Godly, mature men and women in the church
2. Godly, manly pastors and elders
3. Biblically functioning homes

Baucham stresses that each of these three themes represents one leg of a three-legged stool, and each leg is vital in the discipleship-making process.[86] His reasoning is as follows:

1. Godly, mature men and women in the church are those whom Scripture charges with teaching the younger men and women the truths of God.
2. Godly, manly elders provide the example to the flock and leadership within the church.
3. Godly homes are the best place for discipleship to take place as this is where most of life is lived.[87]

Each of these themes uses mentorship as the vehicle through which discipleship is carried out.

Relationships and Discipleship

James G. Samra, in his article "A Biblical View of Discipleship," stresses the importance of relationships in discipleship. He indicates that in the Gospels discipleship literally meant following Christ where He went and learning from Him in a personal setting. It involved learning to suffer with Christ, leaving all behind, seeing what Christ did, hearing what He said,

---

[85] Voddie Baucham Jr, "Equipping the Generations: A Three-Pronged Approach to Discipleship" (Source: Journal of Family Ministry, 2 no 1 Fall-Winter 2011, Publication. ATLA Religion Database with ATLASerials. Hunter Resource Library), pp. 74-79, Accessed 11/5/2014.
[86] Ibid., p. 75.
[87] Ibid., pp. 76–77.

being corrected by Him, and following His example.[88] Samara affirms, "In the rest of the New Testament, because Christ is no longer physically present, discipleship involved imitation of other mature believers rather than literally following Christ (1 Thess. 1:6; 1 Cor. 11:1)."[89]

Samra also says that in the Old Testament there are some examples of what discipleship looked like as carried out in the likes of Moses and Joshua as well as Elijah and Elisha.[90] In all these examples, relationships and mentoring provide the environment wherein discipleship takes place.

Avery Willis, in his article "MasterLife: Discipleship Training for Leaders," stresses the role of relationships in the process of discipleship. Willis states, "Discipleship is accomplished through the practice of basic Christian disciplines under the guidance of mature, practicing disciplers . . . and is carried out in the context of a small group of approximately eight persons."[91] Willis' model uses mentoring as a key component of effective discipleship.

Conclusion

The example of Christ and other mentoring relationships in Scripture highlight the importance mentoring plays in discipleship. For this reason, it's one of the essential components needed in the discipleship-making process. Many affirm that we learn more by observing than by hearing. The mentoring relationship puts this truth into practice as it allows us to see the truth of Scripture lived out and applied to real life.

---

[88] James G. Samra, "A Biblical View of Discipleship" (Bibliotheca Sacra: 219-34. Publication Type: Article, Database: ATLA Religion Database with ATLASerials. Hunter Resource Library), p. 222, Accessed 11/5/2014.
[89] Ibid., p. 224.
[90] Ibid., pp. 226–227.
[91] Avery T. Willis Jr, "MasterLife: Discipleship Training for Leaders" (Source: Theological Educator, no 28 Spr 1984, p 3-5. Publication Type: Article. Subjects: Baptists--Education; Christian life ATLA Religion Database with ATLASerials. Hunter Resource Library), p. 3, Accessed 11/5/2014.

Step 2: Measuring Your Level of Spiritual Maturity in Mentoring

Self-Assessment Test for Mentoring

Please take a moment to answer the following 10 questions to discover your spiritual maturity level regarding mentoring. Answer each question using the following response options. Mark down your points earned for each question and then tally them up at the end to see your level of spiritual maturity in this category. As you take the test, avoid rushing. Answer the questions prayerfully and honestly. After you've taken the test, you might ask a loved one to take it for you as well. This will give you a broader perspective.

Points Possible per Answer

Never...................... 0 Points
Rarely .... 2 Points
Occasionally .... 4 Points
Frequently.............. 6 Points
Almost Always ...... 8 Points
Habitually.............. 10 Points

1. Currently, I am mentoring someone.   _____

2. Currently, someone is mentoring me.   _____

3. I have close friends who I allow to hold me
   accountable for spiritual growth.   _____

4. I listen to feedback from others with open arms.   _____

5. I am careful to admit my errors and ask forgiveness promptly when I've offended others. _____

6. I respond well to criticism. _____

7. I am skillful in teaching and mentoring others. _____

8. I know exactly what to teach others in mentorship. _____

9. I model what I teach. _____

10. I know God's Word thoroughly in order to give counsel and wisdom to those I teach. _____

Total Score _____

Now check your score against the following chart to determine your spiritual maturity level for mentoring.

Spiritual Maturity Grade from the "Mentoring" Test

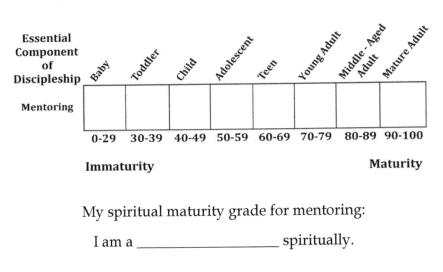

Essential Component of Discipleship	Baby	Toddler	Child	Adolescent	Teen	Young Adult	Middle-Aged Adult	Mature Adult
Mentoring								
	0-29	30-39	40-49	50-59	60-69	70-79	80-89	90-100

Immaturity   Maturity

My spiritual maturity grade for mentoring:

I am a _____ spiritually.

Step 3: Discussion Questions

1. Discuss the meaning of 2 Timothy 2:2.

2. Discuss the meaning of Philippians 4:9.

3. Discuss your level of spiritual maturity in mentoring and why you're at this level.

4. Discuss the meaning of mentoring.

5. Discuss the role of mentoring in the discipleship process and why it's so important.

6. Discuss the role of mentoring in the life of Christ.

7. Discuss the ways in which mentoring can take place in our lives and the church.

8. Discuss which of the following ideas in step 4 you plan on putting into practice and the goals you hope to achieve.

Step 4: Ideas for Growing in Mentoring

Biblical mentoring is an informal relationship wherein a more spiritually mature person teaches and models godly, life-skills to others who are generally less spiritually mature. Mentoring can be formal, informal, take place in a group setting, take place in an individual setting, can be regular, or somewhat sporadic.

Examples of mentoring include small group Bible studies, Sunday School classes, youth group, one on one discipleship studies, accountability partners, and so on.

It should be noted, however, that the most effective mentoring takes place in a one on one setting, or in a small group where specific truths and life-skills are intentionally passed on. The following are ideas to consider for mentoring:

1. Pray that God would lead you to someone He desires for you to mentor.
2. Pray that God might lead you to someone who can be your mentor.
3. Develop a discipleship plan of the essential components you would use in mentoring someone (maybe this book would provide this for you).
4. Develop your own spiritual maturity so you can be a mentor who honors God and models what you plan on teaching.
5. Develop your understanding of what a good mentor or coach is and be a mentor who:

   - Leads by example
   - Has seasoned experience in order to share skills, knowledge, and expertise
   - Has integrity
   - Listens well
   - Has a good reputation for developing others
   - Has time and energy to devote to mentoring

- Has a learning attitude
- Demonstrates spiritual maturity
- Knows the strengths and abilities of their mentees
- Wants their mentees to succeed
- Communicates hope and optimism
- Provides guidance and constructive feedback
- Is respected
- Sets and meets ongoing goals
- Values the opinions of others
- Motivates by setting a good example
- Is skillful in teaching
- Provides insight
- Is accessible
- Criticizes constructively
- Is supportive
- Is specific
- Is caring
- Is admirable

6. Ask your pastor to encourage mentorship in your church.
7. Ask your pastor if you can start a mentorship program in your church.
8. Offer to teach a class in your church on mentorship.
9. Ask your pastor if you can put a sign-up sheet in your church lobby for those interested in being mentored, and another for those interested in mentoring.
10. Ask your pastor if he might preach about the role of mentorship in the context of discipleship.
11. Read books and articles on mentorship.
12. Develop a mentorship guide for training others in how to mentor.
13. Do a Bible study on mentoring.

Week 8: Church Involvement and Discipleship

Step 1: Preliminary Reading

Why is church involvement one of the essential components of the discipleship-making process, and how does God use it to transform our lives and bring us to spiritual maturity?

The Church Is God's Invention

The church is not a new fad or invention of man. God birthed it on the Day of Pentecost, and it plays a unique role in His plan for believers. It consists of both the universal and the local church.

The universal church consists of all those who have a genuine, personal relationship with Jesus Christ: "For in one Spirit we were all baptized into one body—Jews or Greeks, slaves or free—and all were made to drink of one Spirit" (1 Cor. 12:13). The local church can be defined as found in Galatians 1:1–2: "Paul, an apostle . . . and all the brothers who are with me, to the churches in Galatia."

The church is God's caring community where believers find instruction, encouragement, correction, inspiration, and fellowship. Faithful involvement in church helps all believers attain spiritual maturity while a lack of it will stunt a believer's growth.

Church Involvement Develops Spiritual Maturity

"And he [Christ] gave the apostles, the prophets, the evangelists, the shepherds and teachers, to equip the saints for the work of ministry, for building up the body of Christ, until we all attain to the unity of the faith and of the knowledge of the Son of

God, to mature manhood, to the measure of the stature of the fullness of Christ" (Eph. 4:11–13). Christ has given the church gifted men and women for the equipping of believers so that we might all attain spiritual maturity. Therefore, without their influence in our lives, spiritual maturity is unattainable.

Church Involvement Provides Sound Doctrine to Protect Us

In church, we find God's instruction for combatting the lies of Satan and our culture: "So that we may no longer be children, tossed to and fro by the waves and carried about by every wind of doctrine, by human cunning, by craftiness in deceitful schemes" (Eph. 4:14).

Church Involvement Provides Encouragement and Fellowship

Within the church, we find inspiration and encouragement in our Christian lives. As a famous illustration reveals, "A piece of coal removed from other burning coals will soon go out, but a coal left with other burning coals will keep on burning."

Dale Robbins asserts, "Receiving the preaching and teaching of the Word of God increases our faith and builds us up spiritually. Every believer knows what it is to face spiritual conflicts to their faith, and must realize the importance of being fed spiritually so that they can overcome the challenges."[92]

Church Involvement Provides a Unique Visitation of the Lord's Presence

Even though Christ resides in the heart of every believer, there's a special visitation of His presence when believers are gathered together. Consider the following verses:

1. The glory of the Lord filled the Tabernacle Moses built when

---

[92] Dale Robbins, *Why Christians Should Attend Church,* Victorious.org, www.victorious.org/pub/why-church-169, Accessed 10/21/2015.

the people of God were gathered together (Ex. 40:34).

2. The glory of the Lord filled the Temple Solomon built when the people of God were gathered together (1 Kings 8:11).

3. The church was born on Pentecost as believers were gathered together (Acts 2).

4. When persecution faced the early church, they prayed, and the place shook with God's presence (Acts 4).

5. The missionary journeys of Paul and his companions were commissioned by the Lord when the church was gathered together (Acts 13).

6. Doctrinal decisions were made when the church was gathered together (Acts 15).

7. Many of the spiritual gifts are intended to be exercised when the church is gathered together (1 Cor. 12–14).

8. Prayer for healing is encouraged by calling together the elders of the church (James 5).

God moves in a unique way when believers gather, and we experience His special visitation when we're a part of it.

Church Involvement Is an Expression of Our Love for God

Dale Robbins says, "Going to church is a visible, tangible expression of our love and worship to God. It is where we can gather with other believers to publicly bear witness of our faith and trust in God, something that is required of all Christians (Matt. 10:32–33), and where we can bring Him offerings of praise, thanks, and honor, which are pleasing to Him."[93] King David wrote, "I will declare Your name to My brethren; In the midst of the assembly I will praise You" (Ps. 22:22).

---

[93] Ibid., Accessed 10/21/2015.

Being involved in what God loves reveals our love for Him, and God certainly loves the church: "Husbands, love your wives, as **Christ loved the church** and gave himself up for her, that he might sanctify her, having cleansed her by the washing of water with the word, so that he might present the church to himself in splendor, without spot or wrinkle or any such thing, that she might be holy and without blemish" (Eph. 5:25–27).

God Commands Church Involvement

Because God loves us and knows what we need, He commands us to be involved in church for our own good: "And let us consider how to stir up one another to love and good works, not neglecting to meet together, as is the habit of some, but encouraging one another, and all the more as you see the Day drawing near" (Heb. 10:24–25).

Conclusion

In church, we receive from God and others critical components we need for discipleship, and we, in turn, give to others what they need for discipleship. We express our love to God and have the privilege and responsibility to minister to others with our gifts. Moreover, as we engage in this wonderful process, we move toward spiritual maturity.

Step 2: Measuring Your Level of Spiritual Maturity in Church Involvement

Self-Assessment Test for Church Involvement

Please take a moment to answer the following 10 questions to discover your spiritual maturity level regarding church involvement. Answer each question using the following response options. Mark down your points earned for each question and then tally them up at the end to see your level of spiritual maturity in this category. As you take the test, avoid rushing. Answer the questions prayerfully and honestly. After you've taken the test, you might ask a loved one to take it for you as well. This will give you a broader perspective.

Points Possible per Answer

Never .... 0 Points
Rarely .... 2 Points
Occasionally .... 4 Points
Frequently .... 6 Points
Almost Always ...... 8 Points
Habitually .... 10 Points

1. I attend a Bible believing church. _____

2. I have a ministry in my church. _____

3. I have accountability partners in my church. _____

4. I am deeply involved in my church. _____

5. I attend a small group meeting. _____

Week 8: Church Involvement and Discipleship

6. I am open and honest with others about who I am. _____

7. I maintain a clear conscience with others. _____

8. I forgive others who have wronged me. _____

9. I am connected with others in my church. _____

10. I give financially to my church. _____

Total Score _____

Now check your score against the following chart to determine your spiritual maturity level for church involvement.

Spiritual Maturity Grade from the "Church Involvement" Test

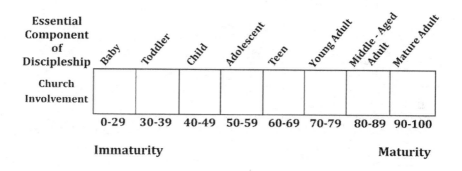

My spiritual maturity grade for church involvement:

I am a _____ spiritually.

Step 3: Discussion Questions

1. Discuss the meaning of Hebrews 10:24–25.

2. Discuss the meaning of Psalm 22:22.

3. Discuss your level of spiritual maturity in church involvement and why you're at this level.

4. Discuss the role of church involvement in the discipleship process and why it's so important.

5. Discuss how church involvement develops spiritual maturity within us as found in Ephesians 4:11–13.

6. Discuss how when the church is gathered together there is a unique visitation of the Lord's presence.

7. Discuss how church involvement protects us from false doctrine and encourages us in our walk with the Lord.

8. Discuss which of the following ideas in step 4 you plan on putting into practice and the goals you hope to achieve.

Step 4: Ideas for Growing in Church Involvement

1. If you can't fully support your church because it doesn't preach or follow God's Word, look for a Bible believing church you can be a part of and support with all your heart.
2. If you're not a member of your church, and they offer membership, join your church.
3. Look for a ministry where you can serve using your gifts and abilities.
4. Pray about starting a new ministry in your church.
5. Pray for your pastor and church leadership.
6. Get to know your church leadership team.
7. Give of your finances faithfully to support your church and obey God.
8. Be more faithful in church attendance.
9. Be careful about being critical and tearing the church down if you haven't been a part of building it up. Tearing down is easy, but building something up is hard work.
10. Commit yourself to loving and encouraging others in your church.
11. Pray about getting more involved in shouldering the load in your church.
12. Apply what you learn to your life. Don't just be a hearer of God's Word, but a doer of it.
13. Learn your spiritual gifts and use them.
14. Be a part of solving problems, not being one of them.
15. Be punctual.
16. Smile, be positive and warm to others.
17. Be friendly by greeting visitors and others in your church.
18. Be hospitable and invite people into your home for fellowship.

19. Read books and articles on church health and growth.
20. Do a Bible study on the purpose and role of the church.
21. Look for someone in your church who is faithfully involved in church and ask him or her to mentor you in this area.

Week 9: Evangelism and Discipleship

Step 1: Preliminary Reading

Evangelism is one of the essential components of the discipleship-making process because it's part of the Great Commission Mandate. It's not just for missionaries in a distant land or those with the gift of evangelism, but for all. Everyone should participate in evangelism in some way or another.

Christ's Focus on Evangelism

The Great Commission Mandate includes evangelism: "Go therefore, and make disciples of all nations, baptizing them in the name of the Father and of the Son and of the Holy Spirit," (Matt. 28:19). Moreover, the corresponding text of Mark 16:15 tells us to "Proclaim the gospel to all creation."

We also see in the life and work of Christ His concentrated focus on evangelism. He was continually calling people to follow Him, revealing the passion of His heart: "For the Son of Man came to seek and to save the lost" (Luke 19:10). If we want to be like Christ, then we must have a passion for evangelism like He does.

We can measure, in part, our spiritual maturity by the level of passion we have for evangelism. If one of Christ's main purposes on earth was to seek and save the lost, it certainly should be one of ours as well.

Unfortunately, the majority of Christians don't share their faith or invite their friends to church. For this reason, Christ would sadly say to many Christians today the same thing He said to those during His day: "The harvest is plentiful, but the laborers are few; therefore, pray earnestly to the Lord of the harvest to send out laborers into his harvest" (Matt. 9:37–38).

Christ Called His Disciples to Be Fishers of Men

"And he said to them, 'Follow me, and I will make you **fishers of men'**" (Matt. 4:19). The same message applies to us today. We are called to be fishers of men. A "fisher of men" symbolizes a person who evangelizes. They have a passion for reaching people with the good news of Christ, seeing them saved, reunited with their Maker, and rescued from sin's destructive domain.

For the person who neglects evangelism, it should give them great pause. How can they claim to love God and others, and care so little about God's passion for reaching the lost? How can they idly stand by as others destroy their lives, head for hell, and not warn them?

Most Christians Are Not Fishers of Men

In research done by Jon D. Wilke, the statistics regarding Evangelical Christians today who share their faith are troublesome. Wilke reveals, "When it comes to discipleship, churchgoers struggle most with sharing Christ with non-Christians according to a recent study of church-going American Protestants. The study conducted by LifeWay Research found 80% of those who attend church one or more times a month believe they have a personal responsibility to share their faith, yet 61% have not told another person about how to become a Christian in the previous six months."[94] Wilke continues, "The survey also asked how many times they have personally invited an unchurched person to attend a church service or some other program at their church. Nearly half (48%) of church attendees responded, 'zero.'"[95]

Many so-called Evangelical Christians are not only extremely

---

[94] Jon D. Wilke, *Churchgoers Believe in Sharing Faith, Most Never Do,* LifeWay.com, http://www.lifeway.com/article/research-survey-sharing-christ-2012, Accessed 08/04/2015.
[95] Ibid., Accessed 08/04/2015.

negligent in sharing the gospel, but many don't even invite their unsaved friends to church. Christ said He would make His disciples fishers of men. However, for many so-called modern day disciples, evangelism isn't even on their radar screen.

Christ Calls Every Believer to Be His Witness

Moments before Christ's ascension to heaven, as recorded in Acts 1:8, He repeated the Great Commission Mandate using slightly different words, "But you will receive power when the Holy Spirit has come upon you and you will be my witnesses in Jerusalem and in all Judea and Samaria, and to the end of the earth."

Notice carefully what Christ said, "You will be my witnesses in **Jerusalem** and in all **Judea** and **Samaria**, and to the **end of the earth**" (Acts 1:8). Another term for "witness" is "evangelize." Christ said some would be witnesses in Jerusalem (their hometown), some would be witnesses in Judea (a little larger circle), some would be witnesses in Samaria (their country), and some would be witnesses to the ends of the earth (foreign missions). Even though they were to be witnesses in different places, all had the privilege and responsibility to evangelize.

Paul instructed Timothy, who apparently was somewhat shy and timid, to fulfill his responsibility in evangelism: "As for you, always be sober-minded, endure suffering, **do the work of an evangelist**, fulfill your ministry" (2 Tim. 4:5). Even though it was uncomfortable for Timothy, he still needed to do the work of an evangelist.

God has given all of us the ministry of reconciliation: "All this is from God, who through Christ reconciled us to himself and gave us the **ministry of reconciliation**; that is, in Christ God was reconciling the world to himself, not counting their trespasses against them, and entrusting to us the **message of reconciliation**" (2 Cor. 5:18–19). In the same way Christ had the ministry of reconciliation (reuniting God with sinners), we have the same ministry as well.

Some feel evangelism is primarily for missionaries or others who have the gift of evangelism. While it's true some might have this gift, it does not alleviate others from participating in evangelism.

We Need to Speak, Not Just Show

A common belief today is that we should let our lives do the talking for us and evangelize primarily by "letting our light shine" before others. This belief does contain truth and is what gives us the right to share our faith, yet if we omit the balancing responsibility of evangelizing through speaking, we are misguided.

If letting our light shine was enough, then Christ, being perfect, would have just shown up, not said a word, and let His "light shine." However, Christ is referred to as the "Word" in Scripture who became flesh and dwelt among us (John 1:14). The spoken word is so important that Christ is called, the "Word." He spent His life speaking and did so much that John concluded his Gospel by stating, "Now there are also many other things that Jesus did. Were every one of them to be written, I suppose that the world itself could not contain the books that would be written" (John 21:25).

Virtually every example we see in Scripture where God wants to communicate something, He uses both a clean vessel (letting our light shine) and the spoken word. We need to be careful we don't allow the fear of evangelism scare us away from sharing the gospel through the spoken word and use the excuse of "letting our light shine" as a reason for not speaking and being bold for Christ.

Conclusion

Believers who are not involved in evangelism are believers who don't share Christ's passion for winning the lost. They are failing to obey Christ in fulfilling the Great Commission Mandate and display indifference to the fact that unbelievers are going to hell. If the purpose of Christ was to spread the gospel, then His disciples today should do the same. Nevertheless, the majority of Christians today are not fishers of men as Christ and His disciples were, and seem to loathe evangelism.

There's a huge disconnect today in the lives of many Christians between what they should do and what they do. The fact that the vast majority of Christians don't share their faith or invite their friends to church speaks volumes about their level of spiritual maturity and devotion to Christ.

Step 2: Measuring Your Level of Spiritual Maturity in Evangelism

Self-Assessment Test for Evangelism

Please take a moment to answer the following 10 questions to discover your spiritual maturity level regarding evangelism. Answer each question using the following response options. Mark down your points earned for each question and then tally them up at the end to see your level of spiritual maturity in this category. As you take the test, avoid rushing. Answer the questions prayerfully and honestly. After you've taken the test, you might ask a loved one to take it for you as well. This will give you a broader perspective.

Points Possible per Answer

Never .... 0 Points
Rarely .... 2 Points
Occasionally .... 4 Points
Frequently.............. 6 Points
Almost Always ...... 8 Points
Habitually .... 10 Points

1. I know each aspect of the gospel.   _____

2. I have verses memorized for sharing the gospel.   _____

3. I share the gospel regularly.   _____

4. I look for opportunities to build relationships with those who don't know Christ.   _____

5. I pray for unsaved loved ones and friends.   _____

6. I am confident in my ability to share the gospel. _____

7. My heart is full of compassion for the lost. _____

8. I am willing to go anywhere to share the gospel. _____

9. I have a heart for missions. _____

10. I am involved in missions by either praying for missionaries, serving missionaries, or by giving to missions. _____

Total Score _____

Now check your score against the following chart to determine your spiritual maturity level for evangelism.

Spiritual Maturity Grade from the "Evangelism" Test

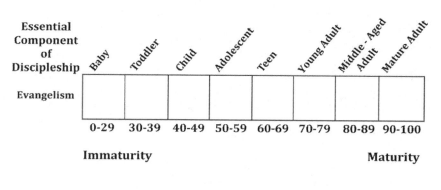

My spiritual maturity grade for evangelism:

I am a _____ spiritually.

Step 3: Discussion Questions

1. Discuss the meaning of Romans 1:16.

2. Discuss the meaning of Mark 16:15.

3. Discuss your level of spiritual maturity in evangelism and why you're at this level.

4. Discuss the role of evangelism in the discipleship process and why it's so important.

5. Discuss Christ's priority on evangelism versus most Christian's priority today on evangelism.

6. Discuss why we're not "Fishers of Men" today like Christ and His disciples were.

7. Discuss how we need to not only "show" but also "speak" in the evangelism process.

8. Discuss which of the following ideas in step 4 you plan on putting into practice and the goals you hope to achieve.

Step 4: Ideas for Growing in Evangelism

1. Write out your testimony about how you received Christ.
2. Practice sharing your testimony with loved ones or friends.
3. Share your testimony at church, in a small group, in a Bible study, etc.
4. Practice sharing the gospel.
5. Pray for opportunities to share your testimony and the gospel.
6. Read and study other Bible verses that focus on the gospel.
7. Read books on apologetics (how to defend your faith).
8. Get to know God's Word better so you are not embarrassed when sharing your faith and are more confident (2 Tim. 2:15).
9. Get to know the missionaries of your church.
10. Pray for missionaries you know.
11. Encourage the missionaries you know by sending them cards, giving them a phone call, etc.
12. Give financially to missionaries you know.
13. Consider serving as a missionary (either short-term or long-term).
14. Read books on great missionaries and the sacrifices they've made for God.
15. Read books and articles on evangelism.
16. Do a Bible study on evangelism.
17. Look for someone in your church who shares the gospel regularly and effectively, and ask him or her to mentor you in this area.
18. Study (memorize if possible) the following biblical presentation of the gospel so you can share it with precision and clarity:

Step 1: God loves us and desires that we would spend eternity in heaven with Him.

John 3:16: "For God so loved the world, that he gave his only Son, that whoever believes in him should not perish but have eternal life."

Step 2: Our sin and rejection of God separates us from Him.

Genesis 2:15-17: "The Lord God took the man and put him in the Garden of Eden to work it and keep it. And the Lord God commanded the man, saying, 'You may surely eat of every tree of the garden, but of the tree of the knowledge of good and evil you shall not eat, for in the day that you eat of it you shall surely die.'"

Isaiah 59:2: "But your iniquities have made a separation between you and your God, and your sins have hidden his face from you so that he does not hear."

Romans 3:23: "For all have sinned and fall short of the glory of God."

Summary of steps 1 and 2: We have lost our relationship with God our Creator, and as a result, have a sinful heart. We do not desire to please God and are selfish and sinful. Our greatest sin is that of not having a relationship with God and loving Him as our Father and Creator. If the greatest command in the Bible is to love the Lord our God with all our heart, soul, mind, and strength, then our greatest sin is not to love and have a relationship with Him. This is our primary sin (Matt. 7:21-23).

Step 3: The price for practicing sin and rejecting God is eternal torment in hell.

Romans 6:23: "For the wages of sin is death, but the free gift of God is eternal life in Christ Jesus our Lord."

Matthew 13:49–50: "So it will be at the end of the age. The angels will come out and separate the evil from the righteous and throw them into the fiery furnace. In that place there will be weeping and gnashing of teeth."

Revelation 21:8: "But as for the cowardly, the faithless, the detestable, as for murderers, the sexually immoral, sorcerers, idolaters, and all liars, their portion will be in the lake that burns with fire and sulfur, which is the second death."

Step 4: God's remedy for our sin is abundant, eternal life through Christ's death on the Cross and resurrection from the dead.

Isaiah 53:5: "But he was pierced for our transgressions; he was crushed for our iniquities; upon him was the chastisement that brought us peace, and with his wounds we are healed."

Romans 5:8: "But God shows his love for us in that while we were still sinners, Christ died for us."

Romans 6:23: "For the wages of sin is death, but the free gift of God is eternal life in Christ Jesus our Lord."

Ephesians 2:8–9: "For by grace you have been saved through faith. And this is not your own doing; it is the gift of God, not a result of works, so that no one may boast."

Step 5: Would you like to receive Christ and His gift of eternal life?

John 1:12: "But to all who did receive him, who believed in his name, he gave the right to become children of God."

John 3:36: "Whoever believes in the Son has eternal life; whoever does not obey the Son shall not see life, but the wrath of God remains on him."

Acts 4:12: "And there is salvation in no one else, for there is no other name under heaven given among men by which we must be saved."

Step 6: How to receive Christ as Lord and Savior.

1. Admit that you are a sinner in need of a Savior.
2. Believe that Christ died on the Cross to pay for your sins and rose from the dead to give you eternal life.
3. Believe that without Christ's payment for your sins you deserve hell.
4. Repent and confess your sins to God, asking for His forgiveness and grace.
5. Pray to receive Christ and His gift of salvation.
6. Give your heart and will to Christ.

Week 10: The Inner Life and Discipleship

Step 1: Preliminary Reading

Why is attention to our inner life one of the essential components of the discipleship-making process? Because what takes place in our inner life is the truest expression of our life in Christ. It's where we apply and live out true spirituality.

According to Christ, an outward focus on keeping His commands with the intent to impress others has no value. He calls it hypocritical and vain: "You hypocrites! Well did Isaiah prophesy of you, when he said: 'This people honors me with their lips, but their heart is far from me; in vain do they worship me, teaching as doctrines the commandments of men'" (Matt. 15:5–9).

Our Inner Life Is the True Mark of Our Spirituality

In the Sermon on the Mount, Christ addresses the issue of the inner life as the mark of true spirituality. He speaks of anger, lust, divorce, oaths, bitterness, retaliation, loving our enemies, giving to the needy, prayer, and fasting, all from the perspective of the inner life before God versus mere external acts done before others to impress them. He warns that merely obeying His commands with the intention of impressing others does not please Him.

Lying deep within our hearts is the tendency to be more concerned about what others think of us than what God thinks. We often strive to impress others by appearing good on the outside but are inwardly different. Many of the spiritual leaders of Christ's day were guilty of this snare as they did much of their service to God solely to impress others, with little concern for what God thought. They were full of pride and selfish ambition.

Unfortunately, we can be the same. Christ recognized this tendency within our hearts and addressed it with a strong rebuke: "Woe to you, scribes and Pharisees, hypocrites! For you are like whitewashed tombs, which outwardly appear beautiful, but within are full of dead people's bones and all uncleanness. So you also outwardly appear righteous to others, but within you are full of hypocrisy and lawlessness" (Matt. 23:27–28). We must take great care to serve with pure hearts that seek to impress God, not others!

The Importance of the Inner Life

Klaus Issler, in his article "Six Themes to Guide Spiritual Formation Ministry Based on Jesus' Sermon on the Mount," emphasizes that the key theme of the Sermon on the Mount is inner heart formation.[96] We can observe that virtually every theme Christ cites from the Old Testament is a clarification of the importance of the inner heart for the New Covenant. Issler sees the segment on the Beatitudes as a further verification of the importance of the inner life in the discipleship process.[97]

Dietrich Bonhoeffer devotes three chapters of his classic book, *The Cost of Discipleship,* to the topic of the inner life.[98] The inner life is where we live, where God knows our thoughts, motives, desires, and goals. When we bypass the inner life and attempt to "go through the motions" or "fake" our spirituality before others, we displease God and worship Him in vain.

---

[96] Klaus Issler, "Six Themes to Guide Spiritual Formation Ministry Based on Jesus' Sermon on the Mount" (Source: Christian Education, Journal Date: September 1, 2010. CEJ: Series 3, Vol. 7, No. 2. ATLA Religion Database with ATLASerials. Hunter Resource Library), p. 370, Accessed 11/5/2014.

[97] Ibid., p. 371.

[98] Dietrich Bonhoeffer, *The Cost of Discipleship* (SCM Classics, Hymns Ancient and Modern Ltd. Kindle Edition, 2011-08-16), Kindle Locations 2163-2398.

Attention to Our Inner Life Protects Us from Legalism

When we neglect the inner life and pursue obeying God's commandments primarily to impress others, we risk the danger of falling into legalism and hypocrisy. For example, some Christians are boastful of their knowledge of Scripture and think they are more spiritual as a result. However, the problem is not that they are knowledgeable in Scripture, but that they have a desire to impress others with their knowledge.

It's the same with all God's commandments. If we do them to impress others, then we have completely missed the mark. This is why a focus on the inner life is so important. Without it, much of what we do can be vain and displease God.

Christ is certainly not telling us we shouldn't obey His commands, but stresses that if we obey them merely to impress others, then we have missed the point entirely. It all begins with pleasing God inwardly, and then we will live our external lives correctly.

The Inner Life and How We Live at Home

Interestingly, how a person lives in the privacy of their home, and how they treat others within it, is also viewed as an extension of the inner life by God. For this reason, God requires those aspiring to be elders or deacons to display their spirituality in their homes before being qualified to be leaders in the church: "He must manage his own household well, with all dignity keeping his children submissive, for if someone does not know how to manage his own household, how will he care for God's church?" (1 Tim. 3:4–5).

The Inner Life and the Lack of Spiritual Growth

God also indicates that if we neglect our inner life with Him, it will inhibit or block our ability to understand His Word and grow. This was a problem with the Israelites and applies to us today as well: "You hypocrites! Well did Isaiah prophesy of you, when he said: 'This people honors me with their lips, but their heart is far from me; in vain do they worship me, teaching as doctrines the commandments of men'" (Matt. 15:5–9).

Similarly, in the Book of Isaiah, God makes a connection between the Israelite's inability to understand Scripture and their lack of attention to the inner life: "And the vision of all this has become to you like the words of a book that is sealed. When men give it to one who can read, saying, 'Read this,' he says, 'I cannot, for it is sealed.' And the Lord said: 'Because this people draw near with their mouth and honor me with their lips, while their hearts are far from me, and their fear of me is a commandment taught by men'" (Isa. 29:11, 13).

This same principle is confirmed again in Christ's ministry:

Then the disciples came and said to him, "Why do you speak to them in parables?" And he answered them, "To you it has been given to know the secrets of the kingdom of heaven, but to them it has not been given. For to the one who has, more will be given, and he will have an abundance, but from the one who has not, even what he has will be taken away. This is why I speak to them in parables, because seeing they do not see, and hearing they do not hear, nor do they understand. Indeed, in their case the prophecy of Isaiah is fulfilled that says: '**You will indeed hear but never understand, and you will indeed see but never perceive**.' For this people's heart has **grown dull**, and with their ears **they can barely hear**, and **their eyes they have closed**, lest they should see with their eyes and hear with their ears and understand with their heart and turn, and I would heal them.'" (Matt. 13:10–15).

Conclusion

If we honor God with our lips, but our hearts are far from Him, we too will struggle to understand Scripture and can even lose the knowledge and understanding of it we once had, thus, becoming spiritually blind. What a severe judgment from God! Moreover, we can displease God and worship Him in vain. This is why attention to our inner life is so important.

Step 2: Measuring Your Level of Spiritual Maturity in Your Inner Life

Self-Assessment Test for Your Inner Life

Please take a moment to answer the following 10 questions to discover your spiritual maturity level regarding your inner life with Christ. Answer each question using the following response options. Mark down your points earned for each question and then tally them up at the end to see your level of spiritual maturity in this category. As you take the test, avoid rushing. Answer the questions prayerfully and honestly. After you've taken the test, you might ask a loved one to take it for you as well. This will give you a broader perspective.

Points Possible per Answer

Never .... 0 Points
Rarely .... 2 Points
Occasionally .... 4 Points
Frequently............... 6 Points
Almost Always ...... 8 Points
Habitually............... 10 Points

1. I am the same in public as I am in private. _____
2. Others can see that God is my highest priority. _____
3. There's nothing in my life I haven't fully surrendered to God. _____
4. I walk closely with God throughout the day. _____
5. I am highly concerned about obeying all of Scripture. _____

6. I replace sinful, impure thoughts with God's truth. _____

7. I maintain a clear conscience before God and others. _____

8. I confess all known sin promptly and ask God
   and others to forgive me right away. _____

9. I forgive others who hurt me and keep my heart
   clean of bitterness and resentment. _____

10. I read and meditate on God's Word to better
    understand His will and keep my life and
    heart pure. _____

Total Score _____

Now check your score against the following chart to determine your spiritual maturity level for your inner life.

Spiritual Maturity Grade from the "Inner Life" Test

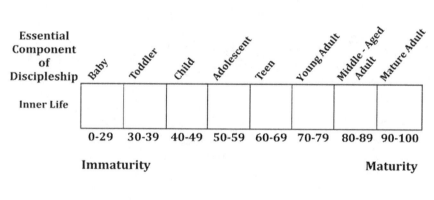

My spiritual maturity grade for my inner life:

I am a _____ spiritually.

Step 3: Discussion Questions

1. Discuss the meaning of 1 Samuel 16:16.

2. Discuss the meaning of Acts 24:7.

3. Discuss your level of spiritual maturity in your inner life and why you're at this level.

4. Discuss the role of the inner life in the discipleship process and why it's so important.

5. Discuss why our inner life is a true mark of our spirituality.

6. Discuss why the way we live at home is a reflection of our inner life.

7. Discuss why neglecting our inner life will cause a lack of spiritual growth in our lives.

8. Discuss which of the following ideas in step 4 you plan on putting into practice and the goals you hope to achieve.

Step 4: Ideas for Growing in Your Inner Life with Christ

1. Prayerfully ask yourself how much of your Christian life and service to God tilts toward looking good before others instead of God.
2. Prayerfully ask yourself if you're more concerned with what others think of you instead of what God thinks of you.
3. Prayerfully ask yourself if you're guilty of the same tendencies as many of those during Christ's day who were hypocritical.
4. Give careful attention to starting or being more faithful in a daily quiet time where you:

   - Pray
   - Read your Bible with purpose
   - Memorize Scripture

5. Do a Bible search for the phrase "selfish ambition" and then meditate on Scripture that speaks of our tendency to be people pleasers rather than God pleasers.
6. Read the "Sermon on the Mount" (Matt. 5–7) that speaks of doing our service to please God rather than others.
7. Ask loved ones or close friends to truthfully evaluate your life to see if you have selfish ambition.
8. Memorize Scripture that deals with pride and selfish ambition.
9. Prayerfully ask God to show you areas in your life where you are displeasing Him.
10. Read a book on the inner life that deals with how you can develop a heart that focuses on pleasing God and being a genuine follower of Christ.
11. Prayerfully ask yourself why you do what you do in your service to God and others. Is it to gain recognition or to please

God?

12. Ponder over your life and prayerfully ask yourself if you have taken stands on biblical truths despite what others think of you.

13. Prayerfully ask yourself if some of your beliefs are held due to what others believe instead of what God's Word says.

14. Do a Bible study on the inner life.

15. Look for someone in your church who displays mature characteristics in their inner life and ask him or her to mentor you in this area.

Week 11: Spiritual Gifts and Discipleship

Step 1: Preliminary Reading

Understanding and practicing our spiritual gifts is another essential component of discipleship. Interestingly, they are not included as an essential component in other lists I researched. Why have I included them in this book? Because Scripture reveals their importance, not only in our own lives, but also in the life of others in the church.

What Are Spiritual Gifts?

Spiritual gifts are special abilities God gives to each believer for their own personal benefit and for the benefit of others. They are endowments that come in the form of grace and special help. They are supernatural enablements given by the Holy Spirit primarily for building up the body of Christ so that all may attain spiritual maturity.

Spiritual Gifts Have Been Given to All Believers

God has given every believer spiritual gifts. These gifts become part of who we are and how we serve God and others. Without understanding and practicing our spiritual gifts, we seriously hinder our own growth and the growth of others in the body of Christ. Ephesians 4:8–15 affirms this truth:

When he [Christ] ascended on high, he led a host of captives, and he gave **gifts to men**. *These spiritual gifts have been given by God to* "Equip the saints for the work of ministry, for building up the body of Christ, until we all attain to the unity of the

123

faith and of the knowledge of the Son of God, to **mature manhood**, to the measure of the stature of the **fullness of Christ**." *And* "Speaking the truth in love, we are to grow up in every way into him who is the head, into Christ, from whom the whole body, joined and held together by every joint with which it is equipped, **when each part is working properly, makes the body grow** so that it **builds itself** up in love" (Eph. 4:8, 12–13, 15).

God has given each person spiritual gifts for attaining the measure of the fullness of Christ, which is synonymous with spiritual maturity.

A spiritually mature person is one who knows their spiritual gifts, and has honed and sharpened them for maximum usage in God's Kingdom. They use their gifts not only for their own personal discipleship development, but in making disciples as well. Spiritual gifts are God's special abilities for these purposes.

No spiritually mature person, therefore, would reject God's supernatural enablement for becoming and making disciples. After all, if the Great Commission Mandate to make disciples is taken seriously, then by default, we must take seriously God's gifts that help us fulfill His mandate. It is, therefore, impossible to be spiritually mature without understanding and practicing our spiritual gifts. For this reason, they are included as one of the essential components of the discipleship-making process.

What Are the Spiritual Gifts?

There are four main passages in Scripture that speak of the spiritual gifts: Romans 12:6–8, 1 Corinthians 12:7–10 and 12:28, and Ephesians 4:11–12. The following gifts are mentioned in these passages:

- **Romans 12:6–8:** "Having gifts that differ according to the grace given to us, let us use them: if **prophecy**, in proportion to our faith; if **service**, in our serving; the one who **teaches**, in his teaching; the one who **exhorts**, in his exhortation; the one who **contributes**, in generosity; the one who **leads**, with zeal; the one who does **acts of mercy**, with cheerfulness." Seven gifts are mentioned here.

- **1 Corinthians 12:7–10:** "To each is given the manifestation of the Spirit for the common good. For to one is given through the Spirit the utterance of **wisdom**, and to another the utterance of **knowledge** according to the same Spirit, to another **faith** by the same Spirit, to another gifts of **healing** by the one Spirit, to another the working of **miracles**, to another **prophecy**, to another the ability to **distinguish between spirits**, to another **various kinds of tongues**, to another the **interpretation of tongues**. All these are empowered by one and the same Spirit, who apportions to each one individually as he wills." Nine gifts are mentioned here.

- **1 Corinthians 12:28**: "And God has appointed in the church first **apostles**, second **prophets**, third **teachers**, then **miracles**, then gifts of **healing, helping, administrating**, and various kinds of **tongues**." Eight gifts are mentioned here.

- **Ephesians 4:11–12**: "And he gave the **apostles**, the **prophets**, the **evangelists**, the **shepherds** and **teachers**, to equip the saints for the work of ministry, for building up the body of Christ." Five gifts are mentioned here.

In total, there are 29 gifts mentioned. However, some are mentioned more than once. Considering this, there are 21 different spiritual gifts mentioned in these four passages.

- **Five Gifts Are Mentioned Indirectly in Scripture:** (1) celibacy (1 Cor. 7), (2) hospitality (Heb. 13:2), (3) missions (Paul's journeys), (4) intercession (Luke 18:1; James 5:17–18; 1

Thess. 5:17), and (5) casting out demons (Matt. 17:18; Mark 16:17; Acts 16:16–18, 19:11–16).

Adding the 21 gifts from the verses mentioned directly in Scripture to those mentioned indirectly, we arrive at 26 spiritual gifts mentioned in these passages.

Are All the Spiritual Gifts for Today?

My intention is not to deal with this question in this book, as time and space don't permit. Instead, my purpose is to simply mention the gifts found in Scripture in order to provide the most comprehensive, extensive information as possible. However, I will provide some clarification that might be helpful.

Those who believe all the gifts are for the whole period of the church are called "Continuationists" (from the word "continue"). Those who believe many of the gifts, but not all, are for today are called, "Cessationists" (from the word "cease").

What Are the Purposes of the Spiritual Gifts?

- **To bring us to spiritual maturity:** Ephesians 4:8–15 states that as each member of Christ ministers to one another using their spiritual gifts, believers are built up and move toward spiritual maturity.

- **To manifest God's presence:** Wayne Grudem articulates, "One of his [Holy Spirit's] primary purposes in the new covenant age is to manifest the presence of God — to give indications that make the presence of God known. And when the Holy Spirit works in various ways that can be perceived by believers and unbelievers, this encourages people's faith that God is near and that He is working to fulfill His purposes in the church and to bring blessing to His people."[99]

---

[99] Wayne Grudem, *Systematic Theology: An Introduction to Biblical Doctrine* (Zondervan Publishing House, Grand Rapids, Michigan, 1994), p. 641.

- **To build unity within the church:** In his letter to the Ephesians, the Apostle Paul encourages believers to be "Eager to maintain the unity of the Spirit in the bond of peace until we all attain to the unity of the faith and of the knowledge of the Son of God, to mature manhood" (Eph. 4:12–13).

- **To reveal our interdependence upon one another:** The gifts are for the building up of the Body of Christ as each member understands and exercises their gifts. We are intertwined and dependent on one another. If one member suffers, we all suffer. If one member is weak, we all are affected (1 Cor. 12:21–26). This can also mean that if one member does not understand and practice their spiritual gifts, then the rest of the body suffers and can be hindered from attaining spiritual maturity.

- **To bring glory to God:** As each member understands and practices their spiritual gifts, the Body of Christ grows, and God is glorified. However, when believers are ignorant of their gifts or do not practice them, then God's glory is diminished in the church, and the Body of Christ suffers.

For these reasons, understanding and practicing our spiritual gifts is one of the essential components of the discipleship-making process.

The Need to Develop and Sharpen Our Spiritual Gifts

Not only should we know what our spiritual gifts are, but we should also develop and sharpen them so that we become masters at using them. The Apostle Paul said he was a master builder: "According to the grace of God given to me, like a **skilled master builder** I laid a foundation, and someone else is building upon it. Let each one take care how he builds upon it. For no one can lay a foundation other than that which is laid, which is Jesus Christ" (1

Cor. 3:10–11).

Paul was a skilled master builder. He had honed and sharpened his gifts and abilities in order to be the most effective tool as possible in the hands of God. He was extremely knowledgeable in God's Word, had impeccable character, was self-disciplined, hardworking, willing to suffer, persevered, and was completely devoted to the Kingdom of God and its advancement. We too should strive to be like Paul and become skilled master builders who know our gifts and use them with precision and excellence.

Conclusion

God has given each person spiritual gifts for attaining the measure of the fullness of Christ, which is synonymous with spiritual maturity.

A spiritually mature person is one who knows their spiritual gifts, and has honed and sharpened them for maximum usage in God's Kingdom. They use their gifts not only for their own personal discipleship development, but in making disciples as well. Spiritual gifts are God's special abilities for these purposes.

No spiritually mature person, therefore, would reject God's supernatural enablement for becoming and making disciples. After all, if the Great Commission Mandate to make disciples is taken seriously, then by default, we must take seriously God's gifts that help us fulfill His mandate. It is, therefore, impossible to be spiritually mature without understanding and practicing our spiritual gifts.

Step 2: Measuring Your Level of Spiritual Maturity in Spiritual Gifts

Self-Assessment Test for Spiritual Gifts

Please take a moment to answer the following 10 questions to discover your spiritual maturity level regarding spiritual gifts. Answer each question using the following response options. Mark down your points earned for each question and then tally them up at the end to see your level of spiritual maturity in this category. As you take the test, avoid rushing. Answer the questions prayerfully and honestly. After you've taken the test, you might ask a loved one to take it for you as well. This will give you a broader perspective.

Points Possible per Answer

Never...................... 0 Points
Rarely .... 2 Points
Occasionally .... 4 Points
Frequently.............. 6 Points
Almost Always ...... 8 Points
Habitually.............. 10 Points

1. I know what all the spiritual gifts are in the Bible. _____

2. I know what each spiritual gift means and how God intends it to be used. _____

3. I know what my spiritual gifts are. _____

4. I am currently using my spiritual gifts. _____

5. I know the doctrinal positions on the spiritual gifts. _____

6. I am a master at using my spiritual gifts. _____

7. I am studying and learning more about how to better use my spiritual gifts. _____

8. I often think about new ways I could use my gifts. _____

9. I encourage others to use their spiritual gifts. _____

10. Using my spiritual gifts give me a deep sense of purpose in life. _____

Total Score _____

Now check your score against the following chart to determine your spiritual maturity level for spiritual gifts.

Spiritual Maturity Grade from the "Spiritual Gifts" Test

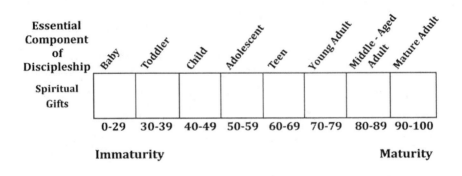

My spiritual maturity grade for spiritual gifts:

I am a _____ spiritually.

Step 3: Discussion Questions

1. Discuss the meaning of 1 Corinthians 12:4–7.

2. Discuss the meaning of 1 Corinthians 3:10.

3. Discuss your level of spiritual maturity in understanding and using your spiritual gifts and why you're at this level.

4. Discuss the role of the spiritual gifts in the discipleship process and why they're so important.

5. Discuss what you think your spiritual gifts are and why.

6. Discuss some of the abuses of the spiritual gifts.

7. Discuss how we can sharpen and better use our spiritual gifts.

8. Discuss which of the following ideas in step 4 you plan on putting into practice and the goals you hope to achieve.

Step 4: Ideas for Growing in Your Spiritual Gifts

1. Do a Bible study on the spiritual gifts.
2. Take a self-assessment test to discover your spiritual gifts (there are many online from which to choose).
3. Take a Bible class on the spiritual gifts.
4. Ask your pastor to offer a class on the spiritual gifts.
5. Lead a Bible study on the spiritual gifts.
6. Write down your spiritual gifts and memorize them.
7. Ask others what they think your spiritual gifts are.
8. Pray and seek out how you can develop your spiritual gifts.
9. If you're not already doing so, offer to use your gifts within your church.
10. Do an in-depth Bible study on your particular gifts.
11. Seek out others who have your similar gifts and ask them to share with you about how they use their gifts.
12. Observe those who are mature in their use of the same gifts you have and watch how they use them.
13. Read books and articles on the spiritual gifts.
14. Read several theological books about the different doctrinal positions on the spiritual gifts in order to understand all views (some believe all the gifts are for today while others believe not all of them are for today).
15. Pray about how you can develop your spiritual gifts in order to be highly skilled at using them.
16. Look for someone in your church who is faithfully using their spiritual gifts and ask him or her to mentor you in this area.

Week 12: Serving and Discipleship

Step 1: Preliminary Reading

Why is serving one of the essential components of the discipleship-making process, and how does it help us attain spiritual maturity? Serving is essential as it fulfills several key purposes for our lives and existence.

God Created Us to Serve

"For we are his workmanship, created in Christ Jesus for **good works**, which God prepared beforehand, that we should walk in them" (Eph. 2:10). The very purpose for which God created us is to serve Him and others. For this reason, serving is one of the essential components of discipleship.

1 Peter 4:10–11 adds, "As each has received a gift, use it to **serve** one another, as good stewards of God's varied grace: whoever speaks, as one who speaks oracles of God; whoever **serves**, as one who **serves** by the strength that God supplies – in order that in everything God may be glorified through Jesus Christ. To him belong glory and dominion forever and ever. Amen."

When we fulfill the reason for which we were created, we find the greatest joy, meaning, and purpose in life. We also bring glory to God, bless others, and bless ourselves.

Christ Came to Serve

After a dispute among the disciples about who would be the greatest among them, Christ taught them a significant purpose for His earthly life and ours as well:

But Jesus called them to him and said, "You know that the

rulers of the Gentiles lord it over them, and their great ones exercise authority over them. It shall not be so among you. But whoever would be great among you must be your **servant**, and whoever would be first among you must be your **slave**, even as the Son of Man came not to be served but to **serve**, and to give his life as a ransom for many'" (Matt. 20:25–28).

Christ came to serve … and did so to such a degree that He died on a cross in His service to us.

Christ also illustrated the example of serving when He, being the Creator of the universe, humbled Himself and washed the feet of the disciples:

When he had washed their feet and put on his outer garments and resumed his place, he said to them, "Do you understand what I have done to you? You call me Teacher and Lord, and you are right, for so I am. If I then, your Lord and Teacher, have washed your feet, you also ought to wash one another's feet. For I have given you an example, that you also should do just as I have done to you. Truly, truly, I say to you, a servant is not greater than his master, nor is a messenger greater than the one who sent him. If you know these things, blessed are you if you do them" (John 13:12–17).

If the purpose of God is that we would be transformed to become like Christ, then serving would rank as essential as it's who Christ is in His nature. If we want to be like Christ, then we must learn to serve as He does.

Laziness and Pride: the Enemies of Serving

God has nothing positive to say about laziness and pride as they kill a serving spirit. Key themes in the Book of Proverbs are warnings about the negative effects of laziness and pride. Both attitudes are self-seeking and end in ruin. Instead, God commands that we develop a servant's heart like Christ: "Do nothing from selfish ambition or conceit, but in humility count others more significant than yourselves. Let each of you look not only to his own interests, but also to the interests of others" (Phil. 2:3–4). He then gives us an example in Christ:

> Have this mind among yourselves, which is yours in Christ Jesus, who, though he was in the form of God, did not count equality with God a thing to be grasped, but emptied himself, by taking the form of a servant, being born in the likeness of men. And being found in human form, he humbled himself by becoming obedient to the point of death, even death on a cross (Phil. 2:5–8).

Christ was a servant, and He calls us to be one too. Laziness and pride must be resisted, and in their place, a servant's spirit developed.

Those who serve God and others will be honored: "If anyone **serves** me, he must follow me; and where I am, there will my servant be also. If anyone **serves** me, the Father will honor him" (John 12:26). What greater honor could one attain than that of the Father?

Conclusion

In the same way Christ is a servant, God created us to serve as well. When we fulfill the purpose for which we were created, we find the greatest joy, meaning, and purpose in life. We bring glory to God, bless others, and bless ourselves. However, the world says just the opposite. It says fulfillment is found in being served. It says power, prestige, and pride define greatness, not humility and servanthood.

Instead of following the world's self-serving attitude, we need to follow Christ's other-serving attitude. Spiritual maturity is other-serving; spiritual immaturity is self-serving.

Step 2: Measuring Your Level of Spiritual Maturity in Serving

Self-Assessment Test for Serving

Please take a moment to answer the following 10 questions to discover your spiritual maturity level regarding serving. Answer each question using the following response options. Mark down your points earned for each question and then tally them up at the end to see your level of spiritual maturity in this category. As you take the test, avoid rushing. Answer the questions prayerfully and honestly. After you've taken the test, you might ask a loved one to take it for you as well. This will give you a broader perspective.

Points Possible per Answer

Never .... 0 Points
Rarely .... 2 Points
Occasionally .... 4 Points
Frequently.............. 6 Points
Almost Always ...... 8 Points
Habitually .... 10 Points

1. I have a ministry where I serve God and others.   ____

2. I am a serving person.   ____

3. I enjoy meeting the needs of others without expecting anything in return.   ____

4. I see my painful experiences as gifts from God to better serve others.   ____

5. I serve God and others through prayer.   ____

6. Those close to me would say that my life is more about giving than receiving. _____

7. I am sensitive to the needs of others. _____

8. I volunteer my time on a regular basis. _____

9. Meeting the needs of others gives me great joy and purpose in life. _____

10. I feel deep compassion for those in need. _____

Total Score _____

Now check your score against the following chart to determine your spiritual maturity level for serving.

Spiritual Maturity Grade from the "Serving" Test

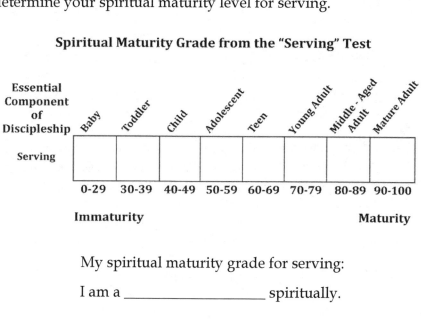

My spiritual maturity grade for serving:

I am a _____ spiritually.

Step 3: Discussion Questions

1. Discuss the meaning of Matthew 20:25–28.

2. Discuss the meaning of John 13:12–16.

3. Discuss your level of spiritual maturity in serving and why you're at this level.

4. Discuss the role of serving in the discipleship process and why it's so important.

5. Discuss why God created us to serve.

6. Discuss the ways Christ served.

7. Discuss why laziness and pride are the enemies of serving.

8. Discuss which of the following ideas in step 4 you plan on putting into practice and the goals you hope to achieve.

Step 4: Ideas for Growing in Serving

1. Memorize Matthew 20:25–28 and Philippians 2:5–8.
2. Ask God to reveal where you lack a servant's heart.
3. Ask God to give you eyes to see the needs around you.
4. Prayerfully reflect on your desires to lead, and ask yourself if there might be selfish ambition on your part.
5. Instead of focusing on your needs, consider listening more and focusing on the needs of others.
6. If you're not already serving in your church, look for opportunities to get involved.
7. Learn what your spiritual gifts are so you know best how to serve God and others.
8. Pray about the needs of your church and consider talking with your pastor about how to meet those needs.
9. Read Christian books on serving.
10. Sacrifice one hour this week to serve in your church or neighborhood.
11. Look for ways you can serve those in your family.
12. Choose to do a random act of kindness for someone each day this week.
13. Ask for feedback on how you could be a better servant from your pastor, family, and close friends.
14. Ask your neighbors if they need help with something.
15. Look for widows or the elderly who might need a helping hand with projects around their home.
16. Serve on a short-term mission trip this year.
17. Serve someone by discipling and mentoring them.
18. Visit the sick in hospitals.
19. Visit shut-ins, the elderly, widows, etc.
20. Do a Bible study on serving.
21. Look for someone in your church who is serving faithfully and ask him or her to mentor you in this area.

Week 13: Spiritual Attitudes and Discipleship

Step 1: Preliminary Reading

Spiritual attitudes have largely been overlooked in discipleship today. Why are they so important that they would be included as an essential component of discipleship?

Many years ago, I was involved in a children's ministry program in the church I attended and was continually puzzled by the leader's poor attitudes. She had been a believer for many years, was knowledgeable in Scripture, and appeared to be spiritually mature. Yet, she was grumpy, rude, harsh, and unpleasant. I wrestled with how this could be. As a young believer, it was all so conflictive to me. How could she overlook a major theme of Scripture, and why would her church put her in a leadership position having such great deficiencies in her attitudes?

Defining Attitudes

Attitudes can be defined as a mental state of mind, a way of thinking, a feeling, a way of behaving, a disposition, a demeanor, or an emotional state of being. Attitudes can be both positive and negative. They are the expression of our inner thoughts, feelings, emotions, beliefs, and values. Without exception, we always have some kind of an attitude.

Attitudes are the living outflow of our lives and always manifest themselves in a certain action or behavior. We will act a certain way depending on what kind of attitude we have at that time. Our attitudes are the reason we do what we do, obey or disobey, or feel what we feel. They are the servants of our will and

140

affect how we interact and treat others.

Biblical Attitudes in Scripture

We see both positive and negative attitudes all throughout Scripture. Galatians 5:22–23 lists several positive attitudes: "But the fruit of the Spirit is love, joy, peace, patience, kindness, goodness, faithfulness, gentleness, self-control."

Despite the likelihood of being in a cold prison cell in Rome, the Apostle Paul's main theme of the Book of Philippians is joy. Not only was Paul joyful, but he saw it as an essential part of our Christian life: "Convinced of this, I know that I will remain and continue with you all, for your progress and **joy** in the faith" (Phil. 1:25).

Philippians 2:5–8 (NASB) tells us to have the same attitude of humility as Christ: "Have this **attitude** in yourselves which was also in Christ Jesus, who, although He existed in the form of God, did not regard equality with God a thing to be grasped, but emptied Himself, taking the form of a bond-servant, and being made in the likeness of men. Being found in appearance as a man, He humbled Himself by becoming obedient to the point of death, even death on a cross."

Jesus also demonstrated the role of spiritual attitudes in His life. One author has noted, "He maintained a perfect attitude in every situation because He prayed about everything and worried about nothing. Jesus' attitude was never to become defensive, discouraged, or depressed, because His goal was to please the Father rather than to achieve His own agenda. In the midst of trials, Jesus was patient. In the midst of suffering, He was hopeful. In the midst of blessing, He was humble. Even in the midst of ridicule, abuse, and hostility, He 'made no threats … and did not retaliate. Instead, He entrusted Himself to Him who judges justly.'"[100]

In the Sermon on the Mount, Christ speaks of key attitudes He wants us to possess such as being poor in spirit, mournful, meek, righteous, merciful, pure, peacemakers, and having a willing attitude towards persecution.

Negative Attitudes

There are also many negative attitudes mentioned in Scripture that God commands us to avoid. 2 Timothy 2:3 states, "But understand this, that in the last days there will come times of difficulty. For people will be lovers of self, lovers of money, proud, arrogant, abusive, disobedient to their parents, ungrateful, unholy, heartless, unappeasable, slanderous, without self-control, brutal, not loving good."

Galatians 5:19–21 also mention several negative attitudes: "Now the works of the flesh are evident: sexual immorality, impurity, sensuality, idolatry, sorcery, enmity, strife, jealousy, fits of anger, rivalries, dissensions, divisions, envy, drunkenness, orgies, and things like these."

Attitudes Are a Choice

We have a choice in what kind of attitude we have at any given point in time, and the attitude we choose affects all factors of life.

Chuck Swindoll highlights the value of choosing the right attitudes: "This may shock you, but I believe the single most significant decision I can make on a day-to-day basis is my choice of attitude. It is more important than my past, my education, my bankroll, my successes or failures, fame or pain, what other people think of me or say about me, my circumstances, or my position. Attitude is that 'single string' that keeps me going or

---

[100] Gotquestions.org, *What Does the Bible Say About Attitude?* www.gotquestions.org/Bible-attitude.html, Accessed 10/23/2015.

cripples my progress. It alone fuels my fire or assaults my hope. When my attitudes are right, there's no barrier too high, no valley too deep, no dream too extreme, no challenge too great for me."[101]

Conclusion

Spiritual attitudes have largely been overlooked in discipleship today. Our attitudes are the visible expression of our inner thoughts, feelings, emotions, beliefs, and values. They directly affect how we interact and treat both God and others, either positively or negatively.

All the essential components of the discipleship-making process are linked to our attitudes. We can reach the highest level possible in each essential component of discipleship, but if we lack the right attitudes in each category, we will still be spiritually immature. This truth is strongly emphasized in 1 Corinthians 13:1–3: "If I speak in the tongues of men and of angels, but have not love, I am a noisy gong or a clanging cymbal. And if I have prophetic powers, and understand all mysteries and all knowledge, and if I have all faith, so as to remove mountains, but have not love, **I am nothing**. If I give away all I have, and if I deliver up my body to be burned, but have not love, **I gain nothing**."

All the essential components of discipleship must be carried along and bathed in godly attitudes, or they mean little, or nothing.

---

[101] Chuck Swindoll, *Strengthening Your Grip* (Word Books, Waco, TX, 1982), pp. 205-206.

Step 2: Measuring Your Level of Spiritual Maturity in Spiritual Attitudes

Self-Assessment Test for Spiritual Attitudes

Please take a moment to answer the following 10 questions to discover your spiritual maturity level regarding your attitudes. Answer each question using the following response options. Mark down your points earned for each question and then tally them up at the end to see your level of spiritual maturity in this category. As you take the test, avoid rushing. Answer the questions prayerfully and honestly. After you've taken the test, you might ask a loved one to take it for you as well. This will give you a broader perspective.

Points Possible per Answer

Never .... 0 Points
Rarely .... 2 Points
Occasionally .... 4 Points
Frequently.............. 6 Points
Almost Always ...... 8 Points
Habitually .... 10 Points

1. I display Christ-like attitudes.   _____

2. I am a loving, kind person.   _____

3. I am a joyful person.   _____

4. I am a peaceful person.   _____

5. I am a patient person.   _____

6. I am a friendly person. _____

7. I am a serving person. _____

8. I am a humble person. _____

9. I am a forgiving person. _____

10. I am a thankful person. _____

Total Score _____

Now check your score against the following chart to determine your spiritual maturity level for spiritual attitudes.

Spiritual Maturity Grade from the "Spiritual Attitudes" Test

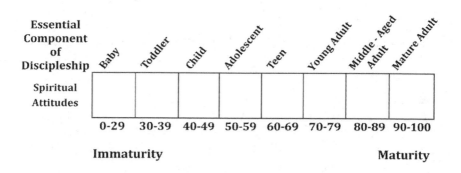

My spiritual maturity grade for spiritual attitudes:

I am a _____ spiritually.

Step 3: Discussion Questions

1. Discuss the meaning of Galatians 5:22–24.

2. Discuss the meaning of Philippians 2:5–8.

3. Discuss your level of spiritual maturity in your spiritual attitudes and why you're at this level.

4. Discuss the meaning of attitudes.

5. Discuss the role of spiritual attitudes in the discipleship process and why they're so important.

6. Discuss the positive and negative attitudes found in Scripture.

7. Discuss how attitudes are a choice.

8. Discuss which of the following ideas in step 4 you plan on putting into practice and the goals you hope to achieve.

Step 4: Ideas for Growing in Spiritual Attitudes

1. Identify your default bad attitudes.
2. Identify the good attitudes that should replace your default bad attitudes.
3. Memorize Scripture that addresses your default bad attitudes.
4. Memorize Galatians 5:22–23, Philippians 2:5–8, Philippians 4:8–9, and Romans 12:9–21.
5. Do a Bible study on spiritual attitudes.
6. Identify godly attitudes mentioned in Scripture that we should develop. Here are some examples to consider: we should be loving, joyful, peaceful, kind, forgiving, humble, serving, encouraging, just, obedient, and respectful.
7. Make your quiet time with God a priority.
8. Ask God to help you identify and change your bad attitudes.
9. Share your desire to grow in godly attitudes with a loved one or close friend.
10. Carefully monitor your attitudes and replace them if necessary.
11. Prayerfully ask yourself why you have certain default bad attitudes.
12. If you are bitter with someone, ask yourself why.
13. Forgive those who have wronged you.
14. Understand that forgiveness is normally both a one-time event and an ongoing process of continual forgiveness.
15. Pray for those who have wronged you.
16. Seek to do something good to bless those who have wronged you (Rom. 12:14–21).
17. Make a list of all the blessings God has done for you and thank Him.
18. Make a list of all the blessings others have done for you and

thank them.

19. Thank God daily for His blessings in your life, even the trials (James 1:2–3).

20. Purpose to smile more, reminding yourself that smiling is a way to serve others, regardless of how you feel inside.

21. Get plenty of exercise.

22. Eat healthy food.

23. Get plenty of rest.

24. Find a prayer partner who you can share your needs with and will be faithful in praying for you.

25. Read Christian, non-fiction books on godly attitudes.

26. Look for someone in your church who displays mature, godly attitudes and ask him or her to mentor you in this area.

Week 14: Character and Discipleship

Step 1: Preliminary Reading

Character is another essential component in the discipleship-making process that has been largely overlooked today, but is foundational to discipleship and extremely important.

Character Is Foundational

In biblical times, knowledge was built upon the foundation of Scripture and godly character. Critical character traits like honesty, respect, self-discipline, diligence, hard work, loyalty, responsibility, etc., formed the foundation upon which knowledge rested.

One of the ways character was taught was by using the Book of Proverbs. It was employed in Israel's educational system, and the study of it was a required subject.

The overall theme of Proverbs deals with character development. Its opening introduction states its purpose: "To know wisdom and instruction, to discern the sayings of understanding, to receive instruction in **wise behavior, righteousness, justice** and **equity**; to give **prudence** to the naive, to the youth knowledge and discretion" (Prov. 1:2-4, NASB). In these verses, wise behavior, righteousness, justice, equity, and prudence are foundational character traits.

I have come to the firm conclusion that character is more important than skills, giftedness, knowledge, social skills, and other important traits. Character is what determines how all our abilities are used, for either good or bad, and is the structure upon which abilities hang.

For example, a person could be extremely gifted musically,

but if they don't have the character of self-discipline to practice, the conviction to produce wholesome music, integrity in their financial dealings, and a commitment to humility amidst success, they will be a total failure, causing severe damage to themself and others. With good character, abilities and knowledge can be acquired, but without it, all of life comes crumbling down.

The Importance of Character in Discipleship

Dallas Willard, in his book *The Great Omission*, speaks of the importance of character in discipleship when he claims, "God is greatly concerned with the quality of character we are building. The future He has planned for us will be built on the strength of character we forge by His grace."[102]

Beverly Vos, in her article "The Spiritual Disciplines and Christian Ministry," refers to the role of character in discipleship: "Through spiritual disciplines one builds great character, and therefore, the disciplines go hand in hand with the power of God demonstrated in one's life."[103]

What Is Character?

Character can be defined as inner traits we possess, aspects of our nature, our moral fiber, and our foundational makeup and essence. It's who we are and what we do in secret when no one is watching. Furthermore, our convictions and decisions are controlled by it.

In Scripture, several Greek words are used interchangeably in reference to character. The following are their usages:

---

[102] Dallas Willard, *The Great Omission* (2009-02-06, HarperCollins, Kindle Edition), p. 124.
[103] Beverly Vos, "The Spiritual Disciplines and Christian Ministry" (Source: Evangelical Review of Theology, 36 no 2 Ap 2012, pp. 100-114, Publication Type: Article ATLA Religion Database with ATLASerials. Hunter Resource Library), p. 113, Accessed 11/5/2014.

1. *Dokimēn*: meaning approved, tried character.
2. *Ethē*: referring to morals.
3. *Aretēn*: meaning a virtuous course of thought, feeling and action, virtue, and moral goodness.[104]

Interestingly, the word "virtue" is commonly used in the Bible when referring to character. It's an old English word translated by some newer Bible versions as "excellence." In Scripture, the word "godliness" is also used when referring to character.

Abraham Lincoln said, "Reputation is the shadow. Character is the tree."[105] Another author has stated, "Our character is much more than what we try to display for others to see; it is who we are even when no one is watching. Good character is doing the right thing because it is right to do what is right."[106] And Thomas Babington Macauley claims, "The measure of a man's character is what he would do if he knew he would never be found out."[107]

Character Is Part of God's Essence

God uses the essence of His character as a foundational reason for trusting Him when making covenants and promises with mankind: "The sovereign Lord confirms this oath by his own holy **character**: 'Certainly the time is approaching when you will be carried away in baskets, every last one of you in fishermen's pots'" (Amos 4:2, NET).

The Apostles Spread the Gospel Utilizing Godly Character

When the gospel was spread to the nations, the Apostle Paul said they brought it with deep conviction and character: "We

---

[104] Bible Hub, *703. Arête,* http://biblehub.com/greek/703.htm, Accessed 10/23/2015.
[105] Character-training.com/blog, *What is Character?* http://www.character-training.com/blog, Accessed 10/23/2015.
[106] Ibid., Accessed 10/23/2015.
[107] Ibid., Accessed 10/23/2015.

know, brothers and sisters loved by God, that he has chosen you, in that our gospel did not come to you merely in words, but in power and in the Holy Spirit and with **deep conviction** (surely you recall the **character** we displayed when we came among you to help you)" (1 Thess. 1:4–5, NET).

Why Is Character Important in Discipleship?

God elevates character as an essential component of spiritual maturity. Notice that virtually every characteristic listed in 2 Peter 2 is a character trait or an attitude:

> But also for this very reason, giving all diligence, add to your faith virtue [character], to virtue knowledge, to knowledge self-control, to self-control perseverance, to perseverance godliness, to godliness brotherly kindness, and to brotherly kindness love. For if these things are yours and abound, you will be neither barren nor unfruitful in the knowledge of our Lord Jesus Christ (2 Pet. 1:5–8, NKJV).

This is a key passage we must take seriously for discipleship. It outlines a process that leads to spiritual maturity and fruitfulness. It mentions three essential components: (1) virtue (character), (2) knowledge, and (3) attitudes.

Developing Character Takes Time

Character is built over the long haul and is not an overnight process. God uses trials, suffering, persecution, and testing to develop His bedrock character within us. He wants us to be like Him, and He is a God of impeccable character.

Romans 5:3–4 says, "Not only that, but we rejoice in our sufferings, knowing that suffering produces endurance, and endurance produces **character**, and **character** produces hope."

James also speaks of its importance when he says, "Count it all joy, my brothers, when you meet trials of various kinds, for you know that the testing of your faith produces **steadfastness** [character]. And let steadfastness have its full effect, that you may be perfect and complete, lacking in nothing" (James 1:2-4).

Peter echoes the same theme as well: "Such trials show the proven **character** of your faith, which is much more valuable than gold—gold that is tested by fire, even though it is passing away— and will bring praise and glory and honor when Jesus Christ is revealed" (1 Pet. 1:7, NET).

Character Is the Main Quality Required in Leaders

Character is so important that it's the primary quality required in elders and deacons: "Therefore, an overseer must be above reproach, the husband of one wife, sober-minded, self-controlled, respectable, hospitable, able to teach, not a drunkard, not violent but gentle, not quarrelsome, not a lover of money . . . He must not be a recent convert, or he may become puffed up with conceit and fall into the condemnation of the devil" (1 Tim. 3:2-3, 6).

How to Develop Character

Greg S. Baker claims, "Building good character is all about addition, not subtraction. What I mean is this: when it comes to change, our focus is usually on the aspects of our lives that are bad. We try to cut out or cut off these negative or bad qualities. We try to improve by subtraction. That is not how you build good character. It is the process of addition in your life that brings the character. In so doing, you automatically take care of the other negative aspects."[108] Baker adds, "The Bible teaches us this concept in 2 Peter 1:5-9. We are to add things like virtue, patience, love, kindness, faith, and so on. It is the process of adding these

---

[108] Greg S. Baker, "How to Build Good Character," SelfGrowth.com, www.selfgrowth.com/articles/how_to_build_good_character, Accessed 12/14/2015.

things to our lives that we gain the character to be fruitful in life."[109] Baker concludes, "So how do we develop godly character in our lives? You practice it until it becomes part and parcel with you. You diligently focus on what you want to add and then practice it until it becomes a habit."[110]

On occasion, however, building character might include ceasing wrong activities in conjunction with building good character. Scripture says that we are to put off our old self and put on the nature of Christ:

> Put off your old self, which belongs to your former manner of life and is corrupt through deceitful desires, and to be renewed in the spirit of your minds, and to put on the new self, created after the likeness of God in true righteousness and holiness (Eph. 4:22–24).

In this passage, we see both putting off and putting on. Therefore, in some situations, we might need to cease certain negative activities in conjunction with building godly character.

Conclusion

Character is a foundational cornerstone upon which discipleship is built. It's part of God's essence and should be part of ours as well. Therefore, we should give utmost importance to developing character, as it's one of the principle components of discipleship. With good character, abilities and knowledge can be acquired, but without it, all of life comes crumbling down.

---

[109] Ibid., Accessed 12/14/2015.
[110] Ibid., Accessed 12/14/2015.

Step 2: Measuring Your Level of Spiritual Maturity in Character

Self-Assessment Test for Character

Please take a moment to answer the following 10 questions to discover your spiritual maturity level regarding your character. Answer each question using the following response options. Mark down your points earned for each question and then tally them up at the end to see your level of spiritual maturity in this category. As you take the test, avoid rushing. Answer the questions prayerfully and honestly. After you've taken the test, you might ask a loved one to take it for you as well. This will give you a broader perspective.

Points Possible per Answer

Never........................ 0 Points
Rarely .... 2 Points
Occasionally .... 4 Points
Frequently............... 6 Points
Almost Always ...... 8 Points
Habitually............... 10 Points

1. I am a person of impeccable integrity. _____

2. I do the right thing when no one notices. _____

3. I keep my word even if it cost me money, time, or inconvenience. _____

4. I obey God regardless of the cost. _____

5. I control my tongue. _____

6. I keep my composure when others attack me, irritate me, or say untrue things about me. _____

7. My motive in life is to serve God with all my being. _____

8. I am a truthful person. _____

9. I am a self-disciplined person. _____

10. I am a hardworking person. _____

Total Score _____

Now check your score against the following chart to determine your spiritual maturity level for your character.

Spiritual Maturity Grade from the "Character" Test

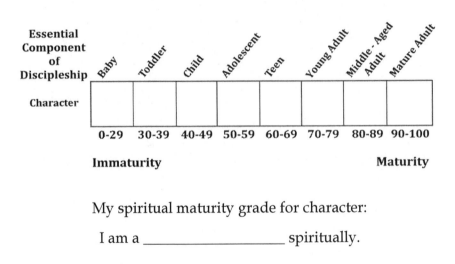

My spiritual maturity grade for character:

I am a _____ spiritually.

Step 3: Discussion Questions

1. Discuss the meaning of 2 Peter 1:5–8.

2. Discuss the meaning of Proverbs 1:1–7.

3. Discuss your level of spiritual maturity in your godly character and why you're at this level.

4. Discuss the meaning of character.

5. Discuss the role of godly character in the discipleship process and why it's so important.

6. Discuss why godly character is a main requirement for leaders.

7. Discuss how we can develop godly character in our lives.

8. Discuss which of the following ideas in step 4 you plan on putting into practice and the goals you hope to achieve.

Step 4: Ideas for Growing in Character

1. Do a Bible study on godly character.
2. Identify godly character traits mentioned in Scripture that we should develop. For example, we should be truthful, trustworthy, honest, loyal, self-disciplined, hardworking, generous, responsible, orderly, cleanly, organized, dependable, faithful, diligent, steadfast, and patient.
3. Identify your character weaknesses by prayerfully analyzing your life and asking trusted loved ones and close friends to help you see your blind spots.
4. Identify the godly character traits you need to develop.
5. Choose your worst character trait and commit to replacing it with the opposite godly character trait.
6. Ask God to supernaturally help you.
7. Practice new godly traits until they become habits.
8. Memorize 2 Peter 1:5–8.
9. Find the verses in Scripture that address your character weaknesses and memorize them.
10. Read a chapter of the Book of Proverbs daily and identify the godly character traits found in it.
11. Read Christian books and articles on godly character, especially ones dealing with your particular weaknesses.
12. Lead a Bible study on character traits.
13. Make a checklist chart of the practical commitments you are making to develop godly character and check them off daily in order to build good habits in your life.
14. Look for someone in your church who displays mature, godly character and ask him or her to mentor you in this area.
15. Persevere, persevere, and persevere! Character takes time and isn't developed overnight. Be patient with yourself and stay committed to it for the long haul.

Week 15: Stewardship and Discipleship

Step 1: Preliminary Reading

Stewardship is another essential component in the discipleship-making process. There exist three main areas in life in which we are given the responsibility to be stewards, and for which God will hold us accountable: (1) how we use our time, (2) how we use our money and possessions, and (3) how we care for and use our bodies.

What Is Stewardship?

Stewardship is the recognition that "The earth is the Lord's and the fullness thereof, the world and those who dwell therein" (Ps. 24:1). Everything that exists (time, material things, the spiritual world, principalities, and our own souls) are the Lord's. They all belong to Him and are given to us to manage and use for His glory and purposes. A steward is someone who manages what belongs to another. They are not the owners; they are managers who are responsible to the owner.

1. Stewardship of Our Time

Our time on earth is far shorter than most people think. Our lives are like a vapor that appear in the morning and evaporate by midday: "What is your life? For you are a mist that appears for a little time and then vanishes" (James 4:14).

King David aptly pointed out: "O Lord, make me know my end and what is the measure of my days; let me know how fleeting I am! Behold, you have made my days a few handbreadths, and my lifetime is as nothing before you. Surely all mankind stands as a mere breath! Surely a man goes about as a shadow!" (Ps. 39:4–6).

Our lives barely register on the timeline of eternity and how we use our time will determine our eternal state. Moses understood this reality and prayed, "So teach us to number our days that we may get a heart of wisdom" (Ps. 90:12). In addition, Moses, "When he was grown up, refused to be called the son of Pharaoh's daughter, choosing rather to be mistreated with the people of God than to enjoy the fleeting pleasures of sin" (Heb. 11:24–25).

A wise person will realize their days are numbered and will invest them in God's Kingdom rather than in the fleeting pleasures this life has to offer. God warned the Ephesian believers, "Look carefully then how you walk, not as unwise but as wise, **making the best use of the time**, because the days are evil" (Eph. 5:15–16).

Christians and Time Management

We live in unprecedented days where voices are screaming at us at every turn, vying for our attention and time. People's lives are extremely busy with countless activities and stimuli. One author has noted, "There's no doubt that the responsibilities and pressures of this world scream for our attention. The myriad of things pulling us in every direction makes it all too easy for our time to be swallowed up in mundane matters. Those endeavors that have eternal value, then, often are relegated to the back burner."[111] The busyness of our day affects how we spend our time and how much we invest in eternity.

To avoid getting lost in the distractions of life, we need to establish goals and make godly priorities. We must make biblical choices and establish firm convictions that become bedrock, non-negotiable commitments, and then do them regardless of the cost.

---

[111] Gotquestions.org, *What Does the Bible Say About Time Management?* www.gotquestions.org/Bible-time-management.html, Accessed 10/24/2015.

We must make the essential components of the discipleship-making process priorities in our lives that we cling to daily.

In chapter 2, we talked about heavenly rewards and how the use of our time in this life will affect the amount of rewards we will have in the next. If we are wise, we will carefully look at how we spend our time. By the statistics we have researched, the average Christian today needs to do some sober soul-searching and reassess how they are using their time.

2. Stewardship of Our Material Possessions

We will also be held accountable for how we spend our money and use our possessions. Stewardship reflects our commitment to God and our spiritual condition. We should never separate money and possessions from our spiritual life, for they are directly linked. How we manage what God has given us is one way of measuring our level of spiritual maturity.

If we use our money and possessions primarily for our own purposes, then that indicates we are still spiritually immature. It matters little how much Scripture we know or how faithful we are in attending church, if we disobey God in stewarding the resources He has given us, then we are still infants spiritually in this area. We see this affirmed in the Parable of the Talents (Matt. 25:14) and the Parable of the Rich Man (Luke 12:16).

Giving to the Lord Financially

A spiritually mature believer should be faithful in stewarding what God has entrusted to them. In the Old Testament, God required a minimum of 10% to be given to Him in tithes (tithe means 10%). In addition to the tithe, the Israelites gave free will offerings, temple offerings, and offerings for the poor. Some have estimated that the Israelites gave around 25% of their income to the Lord in some way or another. In addition to their giving to God, they also had taxes to pay, just like us today.

In the New Testament, we don't see a required amount of money that should be given to the Lord, but rather a principle encouraging generosity:

> The point is this: whoever sows sparingly will also reap sparingly, and whoever sows bountifully will also reap bountifully. Each one must give as he has decided in his heart, not reluctantly or under compulsion, for **God loves a cheerful giver**. And God is able to make all grace abound to you, so that having all sufficiency in all things at all times, you may abound in every good work (2 Cor. 9:6–8).

A spiritually mature believer will be generous toward God, realizing they are His stewards and everything belongs to Him.

If in the Old Testament 10% was the minimum required to be given to God, then certainly in the New Testament He wouldn't expect less. I believe the principle of generosity encouraged in the New Testament would suggest we give beyond 10%.

For the person who fails to tithe and spends what they are stewarding primarily on themselves, God likens this to robbery. This was God's accusation to the Israelites in the Prophet Malachi's day. God said they were robbing Him, which is a serious crime. It's one thing to rob a person, but to rob God is entirely different! That's a crime of drastic proportions. God says:

> Will man rob God? Yet you are robbing me. But you say, "How have we robbed you?" In your tithes and contributions. You are cursed with a curse, for you are robbing me, the whole nation of you (Mal. 3:8–9).

We are not the owners of what we possess, but God is. If we are not faithful in stewarding what belongs to Him, then we can actually be robbing God. If we are faithful in stewarding God's resources, then He will bless us beyond measure.

After accusing the Israelites of robbing Him, God gave them

this promise if they would obey:

> Bring the full tithe into the storehouse, that there may be food
> in my house. And thereby put me to the test, says the Lord of
> hosts, if I will not open the windows of heaven for you and
> pour down for you a blessing until there is no more need. I
> will rebuke the devourer for you, so that it will not destroy
> the fruits of your soil, and your vine in the field shall not fail
> to bear, says the Lord of hosts. Then all nations will call you
> blessed, for you will be a land of delight, says the Lord of
> hosts (Mal. 3:10–12).

3. Stewardship of Our Bodies

A topic neglected in stewardship, but spoken of repeatedly in Scripture, involves how we use and take care of our bodies. God takes this matter seriously: "Do you not know that you are God's temple and that God's Spirit dwells in you? If anyone **destroys** God's temple, God will **destroy him**. For God's temple is holy, and you are that temple" (1 Cor. 3:16–17). These are strong and sobering words — words to be taken thoughtfully! We can debate what "destroy" means in this context, but one thing is certain, it's not positive or something to be taken lightly.

Our Bodies Belong to God

God reiterates the importance of being good stewards of our bodies in 1 Corinthians 6:19–20: "Or do you not know that your body is a temple of the Holy Spirit within you, whom you have from God? You are **not your own**, for you were bought with a price. So glorify God in your body."

Our Bodies Are to Be Used for Good, Not Evil

One way we can be good stewards of our bodies is by using them for good and not evil: "Let not sin therefore reign in your mortal body, to make you obey its passions. Do not present your members to sin as instruments for unrighteousness, but present yourselves to God as those who have been brought from death to life, and your members to God as instruments for righteousness" (Rom. 6:12–13).

Our bodies are to be used for God, not for sin or our own purposes: "I appeal to you therefore, brothers, by the mercies of God, to present your **bodies** as a living sacrifice, holy and acceptable to God, which is your spiritual worship" (Rom. 12:1).

Sexuality and Stewardship

A common way we can misuse our bodies is sexually: "The body is not meant for sexual immorality, but for the Lord, and the Lord for the body" (1 Cor. 6:13). Misusing our bodies sexually is a serious sin that is rampant in our day. Even many Christians are guilty of sex outside of marriage, adultery, and homosexuality.

Sexual sin is unlike other sins. When we sin sexually, we actually sin against and damage our own body: "Flee from sexual immorality. Every other sin a person commits is outside the body, but the sexually immoral person sins **against his own body**" (1 Cor. 6:18).

Dressing Our Bodies and Stewardship

How we use our bodies can also apply to how we dress or mark them. This is important as it can affect our testimony for Christ. In fact, God warns us that doing things that cause others to stumble is unloving (1 Cor. 8). When we dress or do things to our bodies that are extreme or uncommon, then we can damage our testimony and lose influence before others. For example, if we dress in a strange and extreme fashion, then Christians (and non-Christians) may dismiss our attempts to influence them for Christ due to our manner of dress. God wants us to have the widest audience and the largest platform as possible to minister to others.

By dressing in extreme ways or doing questionable behavior, we can lose much of our testimony and influence for Christ.

A trend that is growing widely today is that of tattooing our bodies. There's a verse in the Old Testament I think we should carefully wrestle with before we casually mark our bodies: "You shall not make any cuts on your body for the dead or **tattoo** yourselves: I am the Lord" (Lev. 19:28). While Christians today are not under the Law given to the Israelites in the Old Testament, this verse nonetheless conveys, in some sense, God's feelings about marking our bodies.

I think we should also consider how marking our bodies might affect our testimony as well.

Taking Care of Our Bodies and Stewardship

We also should be good stewards of our bodies by taking care of them. Today, obesity is at an all-time high, over-the-counter drug consumption is unparalleled, junk food consumption is off the charts, and exercise is at an all-time low.

According to recent studies by the U.S. Department of Health and Human Services, many Americans are abusing their bodies. Consider the following statistics:

- More than 2 in 3 adults are considered to be overweight or obese.
- More than 1 in 3 adults are considered to be obese.
- More than 1 in 20 adults are considered to have extreme obesity.
- About one-third of children and adolescents ages 6 to 19 are considered to be overweight or obese.
- More than 1 in 6 children and adolescents ages 6 to 19 are

considered to be obese.[112]

Today, we are abusing our bodies (God's temple) and little thought is given to how God feels about it. We look around, see the majority of people overweight, and think it's the new norm.

Eating and Stewardship of Our Bodies

According to the previous stats, the majority of Americans are not good stewards of their bodies. What does God say about eating and stewardship of our bodies?

God is not silent on the issue and mentions it quite a bit in Scripture. The biblical term for overeating is "gluttony." Interestingly, God frequently uses gluttony and drunkenness together as sinful activities. Consider the following verses:

- **Proverbs 23:20–21:** "Be not among drunkards or among gluttonous eaters of meat. For the drunkard and the glutton will come to poverty, and slumber will clothe them with rags."

- **Proverbs 28:27:** "The one who keeps the law is a son with understanding, but a companion of gluttons shames his father."

- **Proverbs 23:2:** "Put a knife to your throat if you are given to gluttony."

- **Deuteronomy 21:20:** "And they shall say to the elders of his city, 'This our son is stubborn and rebellious; he will not obey our voice; he is a glutton and a drunkard.'"

- **Philippians 3:19:** "Their end is destruction, their god is their belly, and they glory in their shame, with minds set on earthly things." God says a gluttonous person makes food

[112] U.S. Department of Health and Human Services, *Overweight and Obesity Statistics*, www.niddk.nih.gov/health-information/health-statistics/Pages/overweight-obesity-statistics.aspx, 2009, 2010, Accessed 10/24/1015.

their god and has an earthly focus on life.

- **Titus 1:12-13:** "One of themselves, a prophet of their own, said, 'Cretans are always liars, evil beasts, lazy gluttons.' This testimony is true. For this reason, reprove them severely so that they may be sound in the faith."

As these verses reveal, God considers overeating a sin and calls it gluttony.

What Is Gluttony?

One author has commented, "Gluttony is generally defined as 'excessive eating.' In the Bible, the word 'glutton' and its variants are often mentioned alongside drunkenness. Therefore, it's clear that a glutton is someone who eats more than is healthy or eats excessively, and that such behavior is considered sinful. Gluttony is presented as an ongoing practice, not typically as a one-time activity."[113] In other words, gluttony is not overeating on occasion, but overeating regularly, and it's overeating regularly that leads to being overweight.

Why Is Gluttony Ignored Today?

S. Michael Houdmann contends, "Gluttony seems to be a sin that Christians like to ignore. We are often quick to label smoking and drinking as sins, but for some reason, gluttony is accepted or at least tolerated. Many of the arguments used against smoking and drinking, such as health and addiction, apply equally to overeating. Many believers would not even consider having a glass of wine or smoking a cigarette, but have no qualms about gorging themselves at the dinner table. This should not be!"[114]

As mentioned, gluttony and drunkenness are mentioned

---

[113] Compelling Truth, *What Is the Sin of Gluttony?* Compellingtruth.org, www.compellingtruth.org/gluttony-sin.html, Accessed 10/24/2015.
[114] S. Michael Houdmann, *Is Gluttony a Sin? What Does the Bible Say About Overeating?* http://www.gotquestions.org/gluttony-sin.html, Accessed 02/27/2016.

together in Scripture as sinful activities. We are quick to condemn drunkenness but tend to overlook gluttony. No pastor or church leader would be accepted in any church if they were a drunkard, yet they can be a glutton, and no one thinks a thing about it. The straight truth is that we have a double standard. We are biblical in one area and unbiblical in another.

Overeating and Self-Discipline

S. Michael Houdmann weighs in again and states, "Physical appetites are an analogy of our ability to control ourselves. If we are unable to control our eating habits, we are probably also unable to control other habits, such as those of the mind (lust, covetousness, anger) and unable to keep our mouths from gossip or strife. We are not to let our appetites control us, but we are to have control over our appetites."[115]

Consequences of Overeating

- When we are overweight and do not take care of our bodies, we have less energy, strength, stamina, and ability to serve God. Productivity is lowered and money spent on poor health will result in poor stewardship of both our time and money. We also run the risk of dying prematurely, which shortens our time for serving God.
- Failing to be good stewards of our bodies can also sideline us from ministry, causing unnecessary pain in our lives and those around us.
- Being overweight is a symptom of a lack of self-discipline. It communicates to others a message of an undisciplined life. This is especially important for pastors and church leaders to understand because self-discipline is a foundation of the Christian life. When a pastor or church leader is a glutton,

---

[115] Ibid., Accessed 02/27/2016.

they are preaching by their lifestyle an undisciplined and unbiblical way of living to their congregants.

Houdmann asserts, "God has blessed us by filling the earth with foods that are delicious, nutritious, and pleasurable. We should honor God's creation by enjoying these foods and by eating them in appropriate quantities. However, God calls us to control our appetites, rather than allowing them to control us."[116]

Drug Use and Stewardship of Our Bodies

Over the counter drug use is at an all-time high. Estimates suggest 60% of Americans take at least one medication.[117] While much of the medication used today is useful and needed, we can still damage and abuse our bodies by using medication that's not entirely important. Just because a medication might be helpful, doesn't mean it's needed.

Also, it seems many Christians today believe drugs are the answer for all ailments, both physical and spiritual. Anti-depressant drug use is at an all-time high, and the concern is that many Christians are trying to treat their spiritual problems with drugs. I believe we need to be very careful about taking medication for emotional problems.

Our bodies are the temple of God, and He expects us to care for them. His words are quite harsh for those who don't: "Do you not know that **you are God's temple** and that God's Spirit dwells in you? If anyone destroys God's temple, God will destroy him. For God's temple is holy, and you are that temple" (1 Cor. 3:16–17).

---

[116] Ibid., Accessed 02/27/2016.
[117] Jessica Firger, *Prescription Drugs on the Rise: Estimates Suggest 60 Percent of Americans Take at Least One Medication,* Newsweek, 2015, http://www.newsweek.com/prescription-drugs-rise-new-estimates-suggest-60-americans-take-least-one-390354, Accessed 11/17/2015.

Step 2: Measuring Your Level of Spiritual Maturity in Stewardship

Self-Assessment Test for Stewardship

Please take a moment to answer the following 10 questions to discover your spiritual maturity level regarding stewardship. Answer each question using the following response options. Mark down your points earned for each question and then tally them up at the end to see your level of spiritual maturity in this category. As you take the test, avoid rushing. Answer the questions prayerfully and honestly. After you've taken the test, you might ask a loved one to take it for you as well. This will give you a broader perspective.

Points Possible per Answer

Never........................ 0 Points
Rarely .... 2 Points
Occasionally .... 4 Points
Frequently............... 6 Points
Almost Always ...... 8 Points
Habitually............... 10 Points

1. I manage my time well for God's purposes. _____

2. I am heavily invested in building God's Kingdom. _____

3. I am productive and accomplish much for God. _____

4. I let God control what I watch, read, hear, and think. _____

5. I take care of my possessions. _____

6. I am generous with my possessions.　　　　_____

7. I give at least 10% of my income to the Lord.　　_____

8. I am within my weight limit for my body size.　_____

9. I exercise in order to take care of my body.　　_____

10. I eat healthily in order to take care of my body.　_____

Total Score　　_____

Now check your score against the following chart to determine your spiritual maturity level for stewardship.

Spiritual Maturity Grade from the "Stewardship" Test

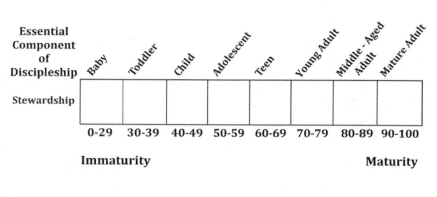

My spiritual maturity grade for stewardship:

I am a _____ spiritually.

Step 3: Discussion Questions

1. Discuss the meaning of Psalm 39:4–6.

2. Discuss the meaning of 1 Corinthians 3:16–17.

3. Discuss your level of spiritual maturity in stewardship and why you're at this level.

4. Discuss the role of stewardship in the discipleship process and why it's so important.

5. Discuss how we can be better stewards of our time.

6. Discuss how we can be better stewards of our possessions.

7. Discuss how we can be better stewards of our bodies.

8. Discuss which of the following ideas in step 4 you plan on putting into practice and the goals you hope to achieve.

Step 4: Ideas for Growing in Stewardship of Your Time

1. Prayerfully reflect on how much time you spend on average on pleasurable activities each week.

2. Make a chart and keep track of how much time you spend watching TV, on social media, on the Internet, doing fun activities, doing nothing, and so on for a week or two.

3. Look at how you are spending your time and make a decision to be a better steward of it, realizing God will hold you accountable for how you've used this precious talent He's given you.

4. Make a choice to say no to the biggest item that is robbing most of your spare time, and choose to do something instead that is profitable and will serve God, others, or develop yourself.

5. Use a "To-do" list to be better organized.

6. Begin each month, week, and day with a planning time to set goals and log tasks that you should do.

7. Organize your life's activities by using a calendar-planning tool.

8. Cut out unnecessary distractions in your life.

9. Get plenty of rest by going to bed and getting up at regular times.

10. Set up a private zone in your home where you can get away to read, study, pray, meditate, think, and grow.

11. Practice not answering the phone, text messages, emails, etc., after a certain time of the day so you can better utilize your time for rest and personal spiritual growth.

12. Prioritize your goals and give more time to the most important ones.

13. If possible, delegate tasks and responsibilities so you have

more free time for spiritual growth and serving.

14. Set a limit to the amount of time you will engage in pleasurable activities per week.
15. Read books and articles on time management.
16. Do a Bible study on time management.
17. Look for someone in your church who is good at time management and ask him or her to mentor you in this area.

Ideas for Growing in Stewardship of Your Possessions

1. Track what percentage of your finances you give to God's work.
2. Make a commitment to give at least 10% of your income to the Lord's work and make it a priority no matter what.
3. Do a Bible study on tithing and giving to God.
4. Read books on financial management.
5. Establish a budget and stick to it.
6. Repair items that are broken instead of buying new ones.
7. Do any needed home repairs that are being neglected.
8. Organize and clean up your surroundings.
9. Commit to getting out of debt.
10. Commit to not spending what you don't have.
11. Cut out needless spending in your life.
12. Eliminate unnecessary spending on pleasure.
13. Read books and articles where faithful Christians have given generously to God and how He has blessed them as a result (George Mueller, etc.).
14. Read Christian books on money management.
15. Look for someone in your church who is good at money management and is faithful in giving to the Lord's work, and ask him or her to mentor you in this area.

Ideas for Growing in Stewardship of Your Body

1. If you are overweight, prayerfully ask yourself why.

2. Commit to getting in shape physically.
3. Commit to a regular exercise program.
4. Commit to eating healthily.
5. Cut out your intake of junk food.
6. Drink water instead of soda, juices, sports drinks, etc.
7. Reduce your eating size portions.
8. Commit to going to bed and getting up at regular times.
9. Find an accountability partner to help you get in shape.
10. Instead of parking close to stores, park far away and walk.
11. Eliminate the poor habits that are causing you to be a poor steward of your body.
12. Read books and articles on how to take care of your body and get in shape.
13. Read the stories of others who have gotten in shape and how they did it.
14. Set clearly defined goals for getting in shape and on how to be a better steward of your body.
15. Do a Bible study on taking care of your body.
16. Make a weekly to-do list for getting in shape that might include the following:

   - Workout five days a week
   - Eat healthier foods
   - Reduce food size portions
   - Cut out processed foods
   - Drink six large glasses of water daily
   - Cut out soda and beverages
   - Reduce or eliminate sweets
   - Eat dinner before 7:00 p.m.

17. Look for someone in your church who does well at being a good steward of their body and ask him or her to mentor you in this area.

Week 16: Conclusion to Discipleship

Step 1: Preliminary Reading

The essential components of discipleship function as vehicles which combine the grace of God and human effort for attaining spiritual maturity. They are not an end in and of themselves, but rather, provide a structure for attaining spiritual maturity. They are biblical, not mere inventions or ideas of people, and they exist to transform us into the image of Christ. These same essential components were used by Christ and the Apostles, and should be used by us as well.

If we practice these essential components with the intent of achieving spiritual maturity, then they will serve the purpose for which God intended. However, if we think that through mere ritualistic conformity to them that we will grow to maturity, then we are greatly mistaken. Christianity is a relationship with God, not mere conformity to a set of rules. Spiritual maturity, therefore, is impossible without the development of our relationship with God.

What Is Spiritual Maturity?

Spiritual maturity is not perfection, but the attainment of fullness, completeness, adulthood, or excellence in each of the essential components of the discipleship-making process.

Christ highlighted obedience as an overarching aspect of spiritual maturity in the Great Commission Mandate: "Teaching them to **observe all that I have commanded you.** And behold, I am with you always, to the end of the age" (Matt. 28:20). Spiritual maturity, according to Christ, is summed up by complete obedience to all of Scripture.

176

The Apostle Peter focused on knowledge, attitudes, and character as essential to spiritual maturity: "For this very reason, make every effort to supplement your faith with virtue, and virtue with knowledge, and knowledge with self-control, and self-control with steadfastness, and steadfastness with godliness, and godliness with brotherly affection, and brotherly affection with love" (2 Pet. 5–7).

In addition to Christ's and Peter's definition of spiritual maturity, the Apostle Paul defines spiritual maturity as:

1. A person who can understand and receive the wisdom of God from Scripture: "Yet among the **mature** we do impart wisdom, although it is not a wisdom of this age or of the rulers of this age, who are doomed to pass away" (1 Cor. 2:6).

2. A person who is mature in their thinking capabilities: "Brothers, do not be children in your thinking. Be infants in evil, but in **your thinking be mature**" (1 Cor. 14:20).

3. A person who has arrived at the measure of the full stature of Christ: "Until we all attain to the unity of the faith and of the knowledge of the Son of God, to **mature** manhood, to the measure of the stature of the **fullness** of Christ" (Eph. 4:13).

4. A person who can discern good from evil through the constant practice of using God's Word, and can understand and feed on the solid food (deep things) of Scripture: "But solid food is for the **mature**, for those who have their powers of discernment trained by constant practice to distinguish good from evil" (Heb. 5:14).

5. A person with a transformed mind: "Do not be conformed to this world, but be transformed by the renewal of your mind, that by testing you may discern what is the will of God, what is good and acceptable and **perfect**" (Rom. 12:2). This verse presents two options for each person: (1) be conformed to this

world or (2) be transformed by Scripture to God's perfect will. Spiritual maturity is the process of moving from the conformity of this world to the conformity of God's will.

A spiritually mature person thinks as God thinks, acts like God acts, and values what God values. They have the same characteristics, attitudes, beliefs, and perspective of life that God does. They are led by the Spirit and submit to Him in all things. They love the Lord their God with all their heart, soul, mind, and strength, and they love their neighbor as themselves.

In summary, a spiritually mature person is someone who has arrived at fullness, excellence, and completeness in all of the 14 areas of the discipleship-making process outlined in this chapter.

Spiritual Maturity Is God's Purpose for Us

As mentioned, it's important to note that spiritual maturity is not the same as perfection. We will never reach that level in this life. However, it's a state of maturity that reflects, by and large, the image of Christ and His values. It's not like a popular bumper sticker that reads, "Not perfect, only forgiven." While this slogan contains truth, it overlooks the majority of our Christian growth to maturity after forgiveness and makes an excuse for bad behavior in the meantime.

Between being forgiven for our sins at salvation, and spiritual maturity, lies a wide gap. This gap is where we labor with the grace of God to attain spiritual maturity. We all begin as spiritual infants at salvation but should not stay there. We are called to much more than forgiveness; we are called to attain spiritual maturity. This is our goal and purpose in life: "Until we all attain to the unity of the faith and of the knowledge of the Son of God, to **mature manhood**, to the measure of the stature of **the fullness of Christ**" (Eph. 4:13).

God's deepest desire is that we would attain spiritual

maturity. In fact, He sharply rebukes those who are slow or fail to attain it as seen in Hebrews 5:11–14:

> About this we have much to say, and it is hard to explain, since you have become **dull of hearing**. For though **by this time** you ought to be teachers, you need someone to teach you again the **basic principles** of the oracles of God. You **need milk**, not solid food, for everyone who lives on milk is **unskilled** in the word of righteousness, since he is a **child**. But solid food is for the mature, for those who have their powers of discernment trained by constant practice to distinguish good from evil.

God was angry and rebuked these Hebrew believers because they were slothful in attaining spiritual maturity. God feels the same about us today! He expects us to become spiritually mature within a reasonable length of time and is grieved when we fail to do so.

God was also grieved with the nation of Israel for the same reasons: "But they obeyed not, neither inclined their ear, but made their neck stiff, that they might not hear, nor receive instruction" (Jer. 17:23).

The Importance of Understanding and Practicing the Essential Components of Discipleship

If the Great Commission Mandate and summation of Christ's ministry was discipleship (Matt. 28:19–20), and if the summation of the Apostles' ministry was the same (Col. 1:28–29), then understanding the essential components of the discipleship-making process is paramount for fulfilling these commands.

God has designed discipleship as the vehicle to bring us to spiritual maturity. That's why it was the summation of Christ's and the Apostles' ministries. The essential components in this chapter are servants of discipleship. They are the nuts and bolts, the specifics, the structure, the application of discipleship for attaining spiritual maturity. They are principles Christ and the Apostles used and work for all people for all time.

A Comprehensive Approach to Discipleship

The premise of this book is that in order to attain spiritual maturity we must approach discipleship from a comprehensive perspective. In other words, we need to grow in all the essential components of the discipleship-making process in order to become spiritually mature.

It was noted in chapter 1 that discipleship has been approached from a single-pronged or several-pronged perspective for much of modern day history, which has resulted in an unbalanced and weak outcome. Themes like knowledge, prayer, serving, and church attendance have been highlighted, while other themes like attitudes, character, spiritual gifts, and self-discipline have been overlooked.

A comprehensive approach to discipleship claims that we need to grow in all the essential areas in order to reach spiritual maturity. Spiritual maturity, therefore, is defined as being mature in all areas, not just a few.

For example, one can be strong in knowledge, but weak in their attitudes or character; this is not maturity. A comprehensive approach to discipleship advocates that we assess each category of discipleship to determine what level of spiritual maturity we have attained, and then give special attention to our weakest areas first. Then afterward, we can focus on all the other areas simultaneously.

Concluding Thoughts

As mentioned earlier, we have many ways of defining success in life today. Some define it as being a sports hero, others as being wealthy, others as being popular and well liked, and still others as being happy. How does God define success? He defines it as being spiritually mature!

Spiritual maturity is our purpose in life, not happiness, pleasure, possessions, prestige, or the fulfillment of our dreams. A lifelong commitment to discipleship is God's will for our lives and is what enables us to attain spiritual maturity. By neglecting discipleship, we reject God's nature and image, choosing instead to retain the image of sin and remain spiritually immature.

Now it's time to look in the mirror and sincerely ask yourself how much you want to fulfill God's purpose for your life in becoming spiritually mature. Today, there is more competition than ever, and most will get distracted with the cares of this life and remain spiritually immature. As a result, they will have few rewards in heaven. They will spend most of their time and energy focused on this life rather than preparing for their eternal home. How about you? Will you be one of them? I hope not! Are you willing to pay the cost to attain spiritual maturity? I hope so!

In closing, I want to encourage you to take some time to truly ponder and meditate on eternity and your life there. Reflect on how fast time is passing and how short life is. Reflect on eternity and its endless essence. Consider others who have passed away and think about how things are for them now in their eternal state, whether good or bad.

The only thing we're going to take out of this life is who we have become in Christ and our service to Him. We need to reflect prayerfully on the stanza from the poem by C. T. Studd that says:

Only one life, yes only one,

Soon will its fleeting hours be done;

Then, in "that day" my Lord to meet,

And stand before His Judgement Seat;

Only one life, twill soon be past,

Only what's done for Christ will last.[118]

May God truly grant you grace and strength as you strive to attain spiritual maturity and lay up for yourself treasures in heaven.

Thank you for participating in this book study and may God bless you for your desire to become spiritually mature!

"So teach us to number our days that we may get a heart of wisdom."
Ps. 90:12

"All flesh is like grass and all its glory like the flower of grass. The grass withers, and the flower falls, but the word of the Lord remains forever."
1 Pet. 24–25

"What is your life? For you are a mist that appears for a little time and then vanishes."
James 4:14

---

[118] C. T. Studd, *Only One Life Twill Soon Be Past*, http://hockleys.org/2009/05/quote-only-one-life-twill-soon-be-past-poem, Accessed 08/27/2015.

Step 2: Measuring Your Overall Level of Spiritual Maturity

Now it's time to add up all the scores from each category to discover your overall spiritual maturity level.

Put your score in each corresponding line:

1. Score from Knowledge of God Test   _____
2. Score from Self- Discipline Test   _____
3. Score from Obedience Test   _____
4. Score from Abiding in Christ Test   _____
5. Score from Prayer Test   _____
6. Score from Mentoring Test   _____
7. Score from Church Involvement Test   _____
8. Score from Evangelism Test   _____
9. Score from Inner life Test   _____
10. Score from Spiritual Gifts Test   _____
11. Score from Serving Test   _____
12. Score from Spiritual Attitudes Test   _____
13. Score from Character Test   _____
14. Score from Stewardship Test   _____

Total score   _____

Total score divided by 14   _____

Now check your score against the next chart to determine your overall spiritual maturity level.

Spiritual Maturity Grade from the "Overall Maturity" Test

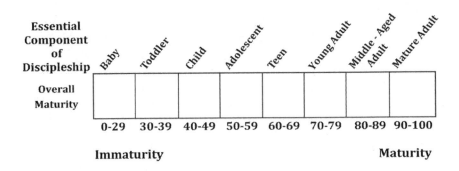

Take your overall adjusted score to find your overall level of maturity in the above diagram.

I am a _____ in my overall spiritual maturity level.

Now look back at the overall spiritual maturity chart and see where you scored the weakest. Next, look at the ideas for that area that you can begin to put into practice for growing toward spiritual maturity. Start with your weakest areas first and then address the next weakest area afterward. Keep doing this for all areas.

Remember, attaining spiritual maturity is a lifelong process so consider rereading this study guide in order to keep growing. You can also read the main book this study guide is taken from (*Biblical Discipleship: Essential Components for Attaining Spiritual Maturity*) in order to get a larger perspective on discipleship and spiritual maturity.

On the following page, an overall chart for each category is provided. This will enable you to get an overall view of your spiritual maturity in each area and measure your progress toward spiritual maturity.

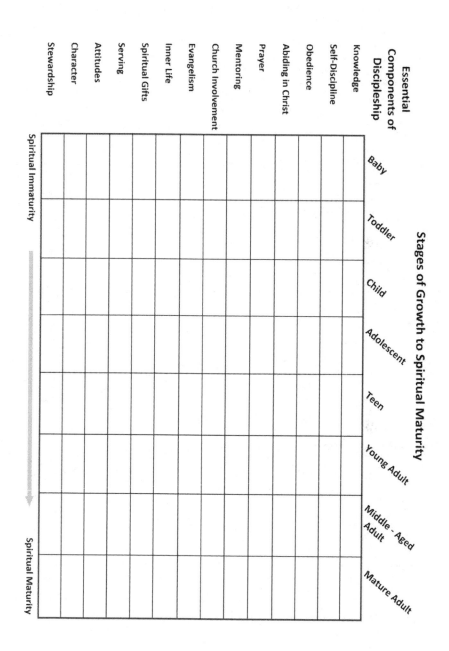

Step 3: Discussion Questions

1. Discuss the meaning of Hebrews 5:11–14.

2. Discuss the meaning of Ephesians 4:11–14.

3. Discuss your overall level of spiritual maturity and why you're at this level.

4. Discuss the meaning of spiritual maturity.

5. Discuss how a comprehensive approach to discipleship is the only way to attain spiritual maturity.

6. Discuss how the world measures success in life.

7. Discuss how God measures success in life.

8. Discuss your future goals and commitments for attaining spiritual maturity.

Bibliography

Baker, Greg S. *How to Build Good Character*. SelfGrowth.com. www.selfgrowth.com/articles/how_to_build_good_character. Accessed 12/14/2015.

Barna, George. *Growing True Disciples: New Strategies for Producing Genuine Followers of Christ*. Barna Reports. The Crown Publishing Group. Kindle Edition. 2013.

Baucham, Voddie Jr. *Equipping the Generations: A Three-Pronged Approach to Discipleship*. Source: Journal of Family Ministry, 2 no 1 Fall-Winter 2011. Publication. ATLA. Religion Database with ATLASerials. Hunter Resource Library. Accessed 11/5/2014.

Beeksma, Deborah. *The Average Christian Prays a Minute a Day; Prayer by the Faithful Helps Their Relationships*. GodDiscussion.com. 2013. http://www.goddiscussion.com/110131/the-average-christian-prays-a-minute-a-day-prayer-by-the-faithful-helps-their-relationships. Accessed 07/27/2015.

Bible Hub. *703. Arête*. http://biblehub.com/greek/703.htm. Accessed 10/23/2015.

Blue Letter Bible. BlueLetterBible.org. *Study Resources: Charts and Quotes*. www.blueletterbible.org/study/pnt/pnt08.cfm. Accessed 10/14/105.

Bonhoeffer, Dietrich. *The Cost of Discipleship*. 2011-08-16. SCM Classics Hymns Ancient and Modern Ltd. Kindle Edition.

Character-training.com/blog. *What Is Character?* http://www.character-training.com/blog. Accessed 10/23/2015.

Christian Prayer Quotes. *Prayer Quotations*. http://www.christian-prayer-quotes.christian-attorney.net. Accessed 10/20/2015.

Compelling Truth. *What Is the Sin of Gluttony?* Compellingtruth.org. www.compellingtruth.org/gluttony-sin.html. Accessed 10/24/2015.

Crockett, Joseph V. *Is There Discipline in Our Discipleship?*
Source: Living Pulpit. Online. March 1, 2014. ATLA Religion
Database with ATLASerials. Hunter Resource Library. Accessed
11/5/2014.

C. S. Lewis Institute. *Sparking a Discipleship Movement in America and
Beyond.* cslewisinstitute.org.
http://www.cslewisinstitute.org/webfm_send/210. Accessed
08/19/2015.

Edman, Raymond V. *The Disciplines of Life.* Minneapolis, Minnesota.
World Wide Publications. 1948.

Fairchild, Mary. *Basics to Prayer.* Christianity.About.com.
http://christianity.about.com/od/prayersverses/a/basicstopra
yer.htm. Accessed 10/16/2016.

Firger, Jessica. *Prescription Drugs on the Rise: Estimates Suggest 60
Percent of Americans Take at Least One Medication.* Newsweek.
2015. www.newsweek.com/prescription-drugs-rise-new-
estimates-suggest-60-americans-take-least-one-390354. Accessed
11/17/2015.

Foster, Richard J. *Celebration of Discipline.* HarperCollins. Kindle
Edition. 2009.

Gotquestions.org. *What Does It Mean to Abide in Christ?*
www.gotquestions.org/abide-in-Christ.html. Accessed
10/20/2015.

_____. *What Does the Bible Say About Attitude?*
www.gotquestions.org/Bible-attitude.html. Accessed
10/23/2015.

_____. *What Does the Bible Say About Time Management?*
www.gotquestions.org/Bible-time-management.html. Accessed
10/24/2015.

Grudem, Wayne. *Systematic Theology: An Introduction to Biblical
Doctrine.* Grand Rapids, Michigan. Zondervan. 1994.

Hayes, Dan. *Motivating Reasons to Pray.* StartingWithGod.com.
www.startingwithgod.com/knowing-god/motivating. Accessed
10/20/2015.

Bibliography

Henderson, Daniel. *No Time to Pray.* Praying Pastor Blog. PrayingPastorBlog.blogspot. http://prayingpastorblog.blogspot.mx/2009/02/no-time-to-pray-no-time-to-pray.html. Accessed 10/16/2015.

Houdmann, Michael S. *Is Gluttony a Sin? What Does the Bible Say About Overeating?* http://www.gotquestions.org/gluttony-sin.html. Accessed 02/27/2016.

Hull, Bill. *The Complete Book of Discipleship: On Being and Making Followers of Christ.* The Navigators Reference Library 1. 2014. NavPress. Kindle Edition.

Issler, Klaus. *Six Themes to Guide Spiritual Formation Ministry Based on Jesus' Sermon on the Mount.* Source: Christian Education. Journal Date: September 1, 2010. CEJ: Series 3, Vol. 7, No. 2. ATLA Religion Database with ATLASerials. Hunter Resource Library. Accessed 11/5/2014.

Krejcir, Dr. Richard J. *Statistics on Pastors: What is Going on with the Pastors in America?* 2007. Churchleadership.org. http://www.churchleadership.org/apps/articles/default.asp?articleid=42347&columnid=4545. Accessed 08/06/2015.

LifeWay Research. *Views on Divorce Divide Americans.* 2015. LifeWayResearch.com. http://www.lifewayresearch.com/2015/08/12/views-on-divorce-divide-americans. Accessed 08/19/2015.

MacArthur, John F Jr. *Church Discipline.* Grace to You. www.gty.org/resources/distinctives/DD02/church-discipline. Accessed 10/08/2015.

_____. *What Does It Mean to "Abide" in Christ?* Gty.org. www.gty.org/resources/Questions/QA161/What-does-it-mean-to-abide-in-Christ. Accessed 10/20/2015.

Martin, Cath. *Evangelicals Admit Struggling to Find Time for Daily Bible Reading and Prayer.* 2014. Christianity Today. www.christiantoday.com/article/daily.bible.reading.and.prayer.is.a.struggle.for.many.evangelicals/36765.htm. Accessed 08/18/2015.

McGrath, Alister. *The Passionate Intellect; Christian Faith and the Discipleship of the Mind.* Source: Pro Ecclesia. 22 no 1 Winter 2013. Publication Type: Review ATLA Religion Database with ATLASerials. Hunter Resource Library. Accessed 11/5/2014.

Mohler, Albert, R. Jr. *The Scandal of Biblical Illiteracy: It's Our Problem.* Christianity.com. http://www.christianity.com/1270946. Accessed 08/18/2015.

_____. *The Disappearance of Church Discipline–How Can We Recover? Part One.* 2005. AlbertMohler.com. http://www.albertmohler.com/2005/05/13/the-disappearance-of-church-discipline-how-can-we-recover-part-one. Accessed 08/20/2015.

Murray, Andrew. *Power to Change: Great Quotes on Prayer.* http://powertochange.com/experience/spiritual-growth/prayerquotes. Accessed 11/16/2015.

Ogden, Greg. *Transforming Discipleship: Making Disciples a Few at a Time.* InterVarsity Press. Kindle Edition. 2010.

Pew Research Center. *Evangelical Protestant.* Pewforum.org. http://www.pewforum.org/religious-landscape-study/religious-tradition/evangelical-protestant. Accessed 08/19/2015.

Platt, David. *Follow Me.* Carol Stream, Illinois. Tyndale House Publishers. 2013.

Rankin, Russ. *Study: Bible Engagement in Churchgoer's Hearts, Not Always Practiced.* Nashville. 2012. http://www.lifeway.com/Article/research-survey-bible-engagement-churchgoers. Accessed 07/23/2015.

Robbins, Dale. *Why Christians Should Attend Church.* Victorious.org. www.victorious.org/pub/why-church-169. Accessed 10/21/2015.

Robinson, Anthony B. The Renewed Focus on Discipleship: 'Follow Me'. 2007. Christian Century, 124 no 18 S 4 2007. Publication Type: Article. ATLA Religion Database with ATLASerials. Hunter Resource Library. Accessed 12/10/2014.

Bibliography

Samra, James G. *A Biblical View of Discipleship.* Bibliotheca Sacra
April-June 2003. Publication Type: Article, Database: ATLA
Religion Database with ATLASerials. Hunter Resource Library.
Accessed 11/5/2014.

Studd, C. T. *Only One Life Twill Soon Be Past.*
http://hockleys.org/2009/05/quote-only-one-life-twill-soon-
be-past-poem. Accessed 08/27/2015.

Swindoll, Chuck. *Strengthening Your Grip.* Waco, TX. Word Books.
1982.

U.S. Department of Health and Human Services. *Overweight and
Obesity Statistics.* www.niddk.nih.gov/health-
information/health-statistics/Pages/overweight-obesity-
statistics.aspx. 2009, 2010. Accessed 10/24/1015.

Victory Life Church. VictoryLifeChurch.org. Intercessory Prayer —
Praying Always.
http://www.victorylifechurch.org/pdf/Intercessory_Praying_
Always.pdf. Accessed 08/19/2015.

Vos, Beverly. *The Spiritual Disciplines and Christian Ministry.*
Source: Evangelical Review of Theology, 36 no 2 Ap
2012. Publication Type: Article ATLA Religion Database with
ATLASerials. Hunter Resource Library. Accessed 11/5/2014.

Whitney, Donald S. *Spiritual Disciplines for the Christian Life.* Colorado
Springs, Colorado. NAVPRESS. 1991.

Willard, Dallas. *The Great Omission.* 2009-10-13. HarperCollins.
Kindle Edition.

_____. *The Spirit of the Disciplines.* 2009-02-06. HarperCollins.
Kindle Edition.

_____. *Transformed by the Renewing of the Mind.* Lecture given
at Henry Center for Theological Understanding, 2012.
https://youtu.be/jkzeUcnzYbM?list=PLApp3jRh1oAqt64uvfw4
J_Ps2lD8bYokR. Accessed 10/15/2015.

Bibliography

Wilke, Jon D. *Churchgoers Believe in Sharing Faith, Most Never Do.*
LifeWay.com. LifeWay Research.
http://www.lifeway.com/article/research-survey-sharing-
christ-2012. Accessed 08/04/2015.

Willis, Avery T Jr. *MasterLife: Discipleship Training for Leaders.*
Source: Theological Educator, no 28 Spr 1984. Publication Type:
Article. Subjects: Baptists--Education; Christian life ATLA
Religion Database with ATLASerials. Hunter Resource Library.
Accessed 11/5/2014.

About the Author

Todd M. Fink is founder and director of Go Missions to Mexico Ministries. He received a Bachelor of Theology Degree from Freelandia Bible College (1986-1990), did studies at Western Seminary (1990-1993), received a Master of Theology Degree from Freedom Bible College and Seminary (2012-2013), and received a Ph.D. degree in Theology from Trinity Theological Seminary (2015).

He served as youth/associate pastor for 12 years at an Evangelical church in Oregon (1987-1998).

Todd (Mike) is currently serving as pastor and missionary with Go Missions to Mexico Ministries in Mexico (1998-present) and is also an author, speaker, and teacher. He has a deep passion for God's Word and enjoys helping people understand its eternal truths. He is married to his lovely wife, Letsy Angela, and has four grown children.

Ministries of Go Missions to Mexico

- GoMissionsToMexico.com ~ Mission trips to Mexico
- HolyLandSite.com ~ Holy Land Video Teachings and Resources
- MinisteriosCasaDeLuz.com ~ Spanish Resources for Pastors
- SelahBookPress.com ~ Book Publishing

Connect with Todd (Mike)

Email: missionstomexico@yahoo.com

Facebook: Go Missions to Mexico

Websites:

- ToddMichaelFink.com
- SelahBookPress.com
- GoMissionsToMexico.com
- HolyLandSite.com
- MinsiteriosCasaDeLuz.com

Look for More Books Coming Soon by Todd (Mike)

- *Biblical Discipleship: Essential Components for Attaining Spiritual Maturity*
- *Discovering the True Riches of Life*
- *Biblical Sites of the Holy Land: See Where the Bible Took Place*
- *Understanding the Fear of the Lord: How to Receive God's Richest Blessings in Your Life*
- *Understanding Heavenly Rewards: An Overlooked Truth*
- *Biblical Leadership: How to Lead God's Way*
- *Gender Roles in the Family and Church: What Does the Bible Say?*
- *Church Discipline: Intensive Care for Wayward Believers*
- *How to Share Your Faith: A Biblical Approach*